NAPLES AMALFI COAST

ISCHIA CAPRI POMPEII CILENTO

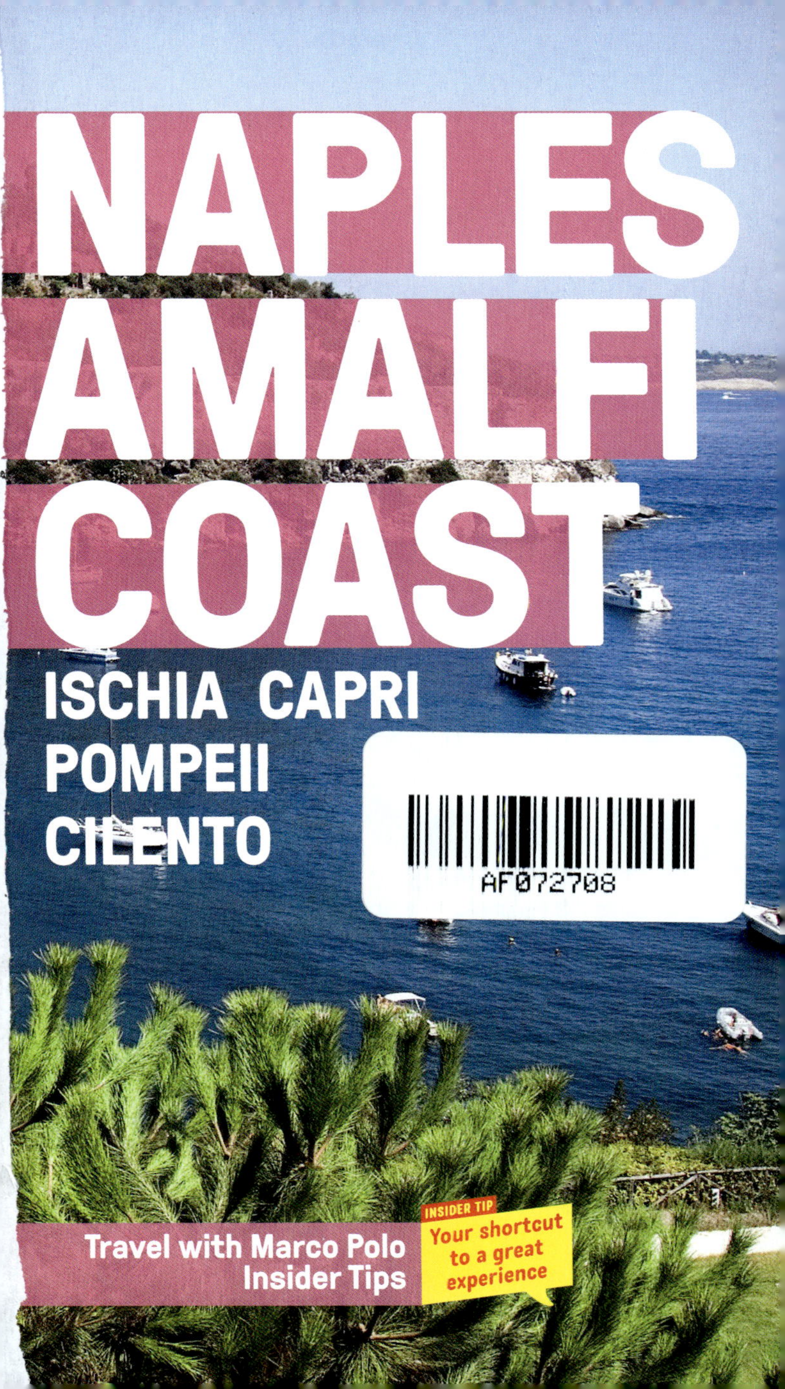

Travel with Marco Polo Insider Tips

INSIDER TIP Your shortcut to a great experience

MARCO POLO TOP HIGHLIGHTS

MUSEO E REAL BOSCO DI CAPODIMONTE ★
Here, the walls are covered in works by international masters from different periods, with Neapolitan Baroque painters taking pride of place.

➤ p. 48, Naples

STAZIONI DELL'ARTE IN NAPLES ★
Take the escalator down to the fascinating art stations of the *Metrò dell'Arte*.
📷 *Tip: Have your camera ready on the down escalator at Toledo station and, when you're a third of the way down, take a photo facing upwards.*

➤ p. 49, Naples

CAPRI ★
This charming island enchants everyone with its beauty.
📷 *Tip: Ten minutes into the boat ride, take a selfie with the silhouette of the island behind you.*

➤ p. 76, Capri, Ischia, Procida

EXCAVATIONS IN POMPEII ★
From today's perspective, the devastating eruption of Mount Vesuvius in 79 CE may be seen as a stroke of luck, because it allows us to witness first-hand how the Pompeiians once lived.

➤ p. 68, Herculaneum & Pompeii

ANTICHI SENTIERI ★
A hike on ancient stairways and mule tracks above Amalfi and Positano shows nature at its most spectacular.

➤ p. 98, Sorrento & the Amalfi Coast

EXCAVATIONS IN HERCULANEUM ⭐

Even better preserved than Pompeii, including charred wooden artefacts and beams.
📷 *Tip: Turn round to the left of the ramp at the entrance, and you will have both the excavations and the new city in the frame.*

➤ p. 65, Herculaneum & Pompeii

CUMA ⭐

In the footsteps of antiquity: impressive ruins bear witness to the presence of the Greeks in southern Italy almost 3,000 years ago.

➤ p. 57, Naples

PAESTUM ⭐

Until 300 years ago, the perfectly preserved Greek temples with their frescoes were still hidden in mud.
📷 *Tip: At night, the illuminated temples look like UFOs from a distance.*

➤ p. 110, Paestum & Cilento

TERRAZZA DELL'INFINITO ⭐

The name is most appropriate: from the panoramic terrace in Ravello, the view seems to extend into infinity (see photo).
📷 *Tip: The best time is roughly 40 minutes before sunset (but keep an eye on the park's opening hours!).*

➤ p. 103, Sorrento & the Amalfi Coast

MUSEO ARCHEOLOGICO NAZIONALE IN NAPLES ⭐

What was important to the Romans 2,000 years ago? This world-famous collection provides exciting answers from Pompeii and other sites.

➤ p. 46, Naples

CONTENTS

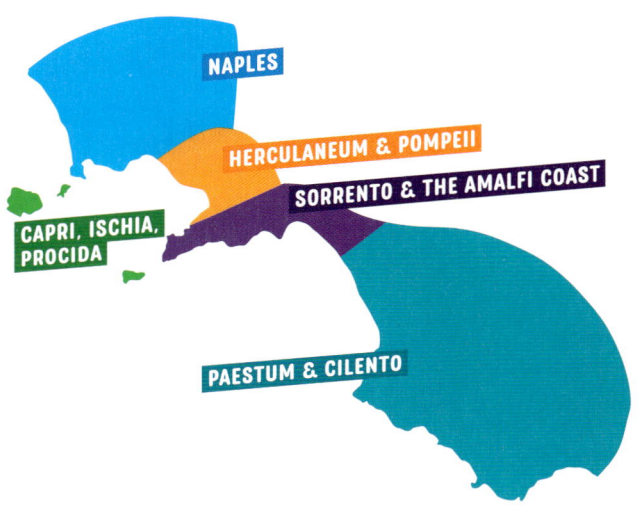

36 REGIONAL OVERVIEW

38 NAPLES
Around Naples 55

58 HERCULANEUM & POMPEII
Herculaneum (Ercolano) & around 64
Pompeii & around 68

72 CAPRI, ISCHIA, PROCIDA
Capri 76
Ischia 79
Procida 82

84 SORRENTO & THE AMALFI COAST
Sorrento & around 88
Positano & around 92
Amalfi & around 95
Ravello 102
Salerno 104

106 PAESTUM & CILENTO
Paestum & around 110
Castellabate & around 112
Palinuro & around 115
Marina di Camerota & around 118

CONTENTS

MARCO POLO TOP HIGHLIGHTS
2   Top 10 highlights

BEST OF NAPLES & THE AMALFI COAST
8   ... when it rains
9   ... on a budget
10 ... with children
11 ... classic experiences

GET TO KNOW NAPLES & THE AMALFI COAST
14 Discover Naples & the Amalfi Coast
17 At a glance
18 Understand Naples & the Amalfi Coast
21 True or false?

EATING, SHOPPING, SPORT
26 Eating & drinking
30 Shopping
32 Sport & activities

MARCO POLO REGIONS

36 Regional overview

DISCOVERY TOURS

122 Golden age around Caserta & Capua
126 Through Cilento's karst landscape
128 Bird's-eye view from Capri's highest peak

GOOD TO KNOW

130 **HOLIDAY BASICS**
    Arrival, Getting around, Festivals & events, Emergencies, Essentials, Weather

136 **USEFUL WORDS & PHRASES**
    Don't be lost for words

138 **HOLIDAY VIBES**
    Books, films, music & blogs

140 **TRAVEL PURSUIT**
    The Marco Polo holiday quiz

142 **INDEX & CREDITS**

144 **DOS & DON'TS**
    How to avoid slip-ups & blunders

⏱ Plan your visit	🍴 Eating & drinking	Rainy day activities
€–€€€ Price categories	🛍 Shopping	Budget activities
(*) Premium-rate telephone number	🍸 Nightlife	Family activities
	Top beaches	Classic experiences

(*A2*) Refers to the removable pull-out map
(*a2*) Refers to the inset map on the pull-out map
(*0*) Located off the pull-out map

BEST OF NAPLES & THE AMALFI COAST

Like many places on the Amalfi Coast, Atrani literally clings to the hillside

BEST WHEN IT RAINS

ACTIVITIES TO BRIGHTEN YOUR DAY

TAKE THE PLUNGE
When it rains, the ocean takes on wonderful colours and feels much warmer. Put on your mask and flippers and take the plunge, for example in *Baia*. But when there's a thunderstorm it's better to stay on dry land.
➤ p. 35, Sport & activities

TIME TRAVEL
Beneath the San Lorenzo monastery lies an excavated shopping street from Roman times: *La Neapolis Sotterrata*, a kind of Pompeii in miniature. With every step you take you can imagine going 2,000 years into the past!
➤ p. 44, Naples

NAPLES UNDERGROUND
Discover the *catacombs*: Greek aqueducts, Roman neighbourhoods, early Christian frescoes and the cult of the dead. Most of these historical sites are located in the Sanità quarter.
➤ p. 50, Naples

BESPOKE BROLLY FOR A STROLL THROUGH NAPLES
If the rain catches you by surprise, you can stay dry and continue your sightseeing tour with an umbrella made by *Talarico*. The family business has been making the finest *ombrelli* by hand since 1860. The shop itself is also fun: fans come from all over the world, and thank-you letters and photos adorn the walls like a small museum.
➤ p. 53, Naples

STALACTITES & STALAGMITES
There is a remarkable karst cave system in Cilento, and the most impressive caves are the *Grotte di Castelcivita*, extensive caverns full of enchanting stalagmite and stalactite formations (photo).
➤ p. 112, Paestum & Cilento

BEST ON A BUDGET

FOR SMALLER WALLETS

STYLISH & COOL
The *Mercato di Resina*, an iconic second-hand clothing market in Ercolano – which was born out of the economic deprivations of World War II and the Neapolitan talent for improvisation – is popular with bargain hunters, styling enthusiasts, and theatre and film costume designers from around the world.
➤ p. 31, Shopping

ART ON THE GO
Internationally renowned artists and architects have designed the *Stazioni dell'Arte* of Metro Line 1 in Naples. So buy your Metro ticket and get the art for free! (photo)
➤ p. 49, Naples

ART & COFFEE
The renowned *Gran Caffè Gambrinus* is a coffee shop and art gallery rolled into one: the walls of the café are covered in beautiful pictures from the most famous Neapolitan artists of the early 19th century.
➤ p. 52, Naples

SPAS FOR FREE
More than 100 thermal springs bubble forth on Ischia, and thermal parks set in lush subtropical gardens guarantee spa and bathing pleasures. Enjoy the hot thermal waters in the sea at *Sorgeto Bay*, which is easily accessible by boat from Sant'Angelo, entirely for free.
➤ p. 81, Capri, Ischia, Procida

CULTURE VULTURES
Viewing old masters and modern art doesn't have to be expensive. With the *Campania Artecard*, you can see exhibitions and collections for free or at a discount (and you can also travel for free on all public transport in Naples).
➤ p. 134, Good to know

BEST WITH CHILDREN

FUN FOR YOUNG & OLD

OSPEDALE DELLE BAMBOLE

This doll and toy paradise is a pure delight for the young and the young at heart. For four generations, Dottoressa Tiziana Grassi's family has been repairing dolls from around the world in their doll hospital.
➤ p. 44, Naples

CITTÀ DELLA SCIENZA

This interesting, modern science museum is on the western outskirts of Naples, on the way to Pozzuoli. The interactive exhibits detail how our world functions: how the cosmos works, how lightning happens and what our bodies look like inside. There's also a section for small children.
➤ p. 49, Naples

VIRTUAL VISIT TO ANTIQUITY

How did the Romans live? What did their houses and streets look like? At the *Museo Archeologico Virtuale (MAV)* in Herculaneum, you can take a virtual walk through a small ancient town.
➤ p. 66, Herculaneum & Pompeii

BOAT TRIP WITH PICNIC

Along the Cilento coast, fishermen ferry holidaymakers from the resorts to the coves and wonderful sea caves. The trips often include a picnic on the beach where the fishermen grill fresh fish. There are also night tours under the stars – a special experience for both children and adults.
➤ p. 116, Paestum & Cilento

CYCLE THROUGH A HISTORIC PARK …

… where royal children once travelled by carriage. Hire a bike or rickshaw in the *park of the Reggia di Caserta* and take a leisurely ride along the waterway, down elegant avenues or through the woods at this "Versailles of the south".
➤ p. 124, Discovery tours

BEST 🚩
CLASSIC EXPERIENCES

ONLY IN NAPLES & ON THE AMALFI COAST

BLOOD MIRACLE & CULT OF SAINTS
Three times a year the blood of *San Gennaro*, Naples' patron saint, is liquefied, to the delight of his devotees. There are countless other saints who are worshipped in Naples.
➤ p. 20, 44, Naples

TUFF ON TUFF
Naples is built on and from the rock known as tuff. Since antiquity, this volcanic rock has been excavated 40m underground and the quarried stone has been used to build houses. The excavation has created a labyrinth of tunnels that can be visited today at the unique *Napoli Sotterranea* museum.
➤ p. 44, Naples

PIZZA, AMORE MIO
Pizza is said to be the world's favourite dish. For the Neapolitans, it undoubtedly is. There are 8,200 pizzerias in and around Naples and every *andiamo-a-mangiare-una-pizza* date is guaranteed to get people in the mood. On Saturday evenings, you may have to queue for hours to get a good table: *Da Gino Sorbillo*, for example, is legendary.
➤ p. 51, Naples

GELATO AL LIMONE
This area is famed for its lemons and tempts with its *limoncello* (photo), freshly squeezed *spremuta di limone*, a *limoncello spritz* or the creamy *delizia al limone* dessert. Enjoy the refreshing and delicious *gelato al limone* in the *Buonocore* ice-cream parlour in Capri!
➤ p. 78, Capri, Ischia, Procida

ENDLESS VIEWS
Panoramic views are always worth the effort. On the high hiking trail *Sentiero degli Dei,* above Positano and Amalfi, you are rewarded with magnificent views all the way from Capri to Cilento.
➤ p. 98, Sorrento & the Amalfi Coast

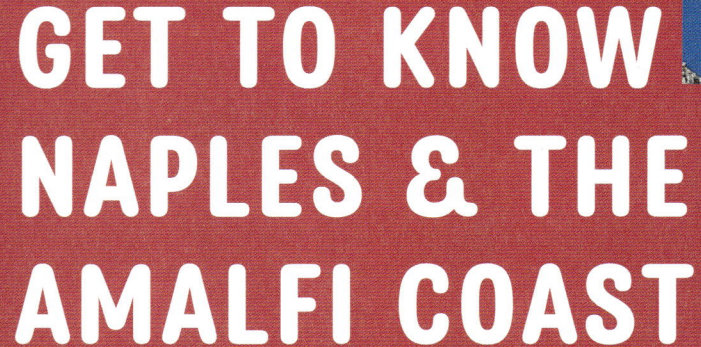

GET TO KNOW NAPLES & THE AMALFI COAST

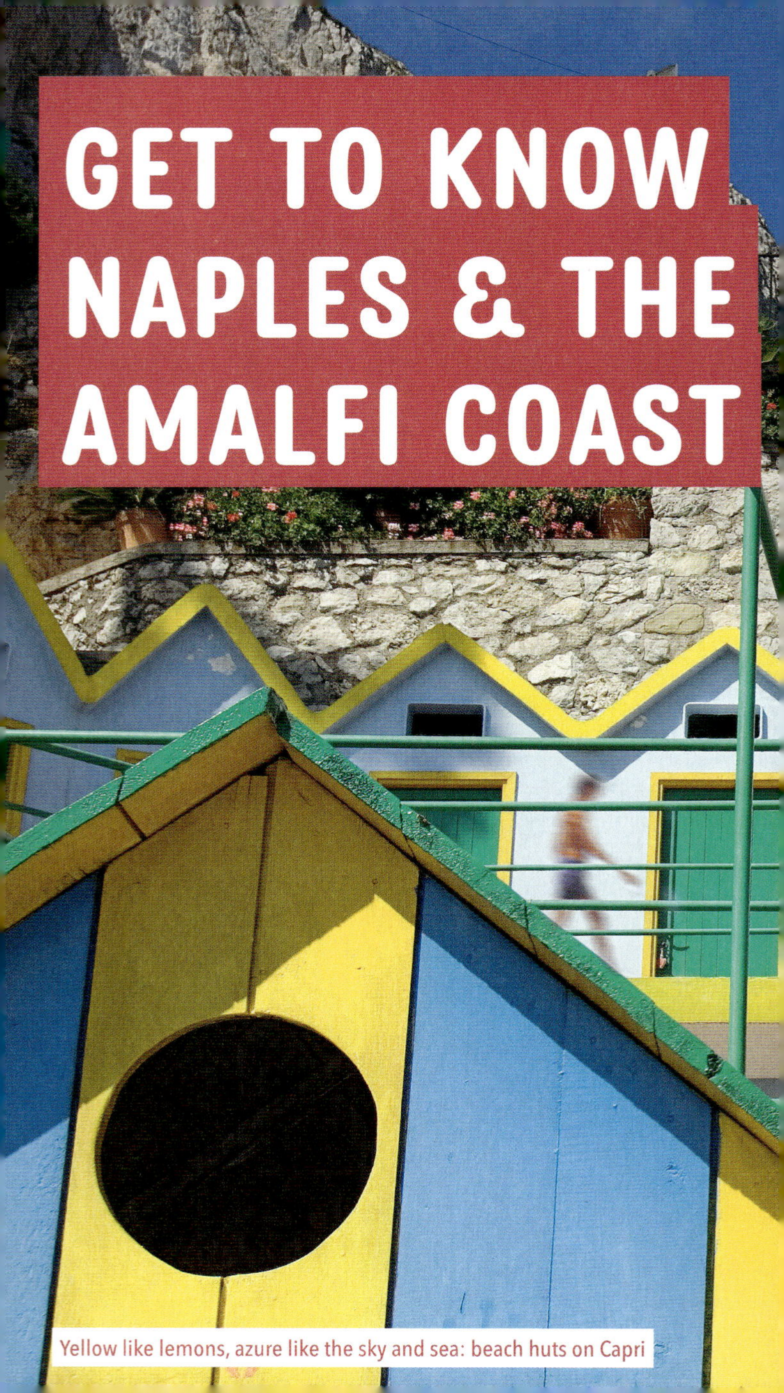

Yellow like lemons, azure like the sky and sea: beach huts on Capri

DISCOVER NAPLES & THE AMALFI COAST

The Calore river gorge in the Cilento hinterland shows a very different side of Campania

No matter where you begin your Gulf of Naples journey, the most beautiful introduction has to be a view over the Gulf: from the Sorrento Peninsula, for example, or from the balconies and terraces of the gorgeous old hotels that rise high above the sea in the town of Sorrento, set on a volcanic plateau.

THE EVER-PRESENT VOLCANO

Mount Vesuvius has always symbolised the city of Naples. The best way to feel that you are really here is to look out over the sea towards Mount Vesuvius. The imposing silhouette of the volcano is most impressive from the monastery of San Martino. On a clear day, you will see Naples, with its densely built-up historic centre, below you, and behind it the seemingly endless sea of houses in the

8th–5th century BCE
Greek colonies develop, one of which is Neapolis, the "new town"

From 4th/3rd century BCE
Romanisation of Greek cities, the Roman upper class build superbly situated villas

CE 79
A devastating eruption of Mount Vesuvius destroys Herculaneum and Pompeii

11th–13th century
Under the rule of the Normans and Hohenstaufen dynasty, southern Italy forms a political unit

1734
Bourbon King Charles III conquers Naples. The excavations in Pompeii begin

GET TO KNOW NAPLES & THE AMALFI COAST

province of Naples, home to more than three million people.

Napule è mille culure, "Naples is the city of a thousand colours", chanted iconic singer Pino Daniele. But other headlines may come to mind: rubbish scandals, bloody Camorra feuds and environmental disasters have left their mark on Naples. They do still occur, but the tide has turned. In recent times, Naples has become one of the most visited cities in Italy. In addition to the old city centre, which is a UNESCO World Heritage Site, and the world-class museums, such as the Museo Archeologico and the Capodimonte Museum, new attractions are enriching the art scene. First and foremost are the stations on Metro Line 1 designed by international avant-garde artists; the new MADRE and PAN museums; the Museo Hermann Nitsch in an old power station; and the Casa Morra art project. Contemporary art is now a permanent fixture in the city.

Despite the tourist boom, Naples has remained a typical Italian city: the historic centre is still inhabited by locals and students, the daily rhythm of the Neapolitans determines the traffic and the background noise everywhere, and the bustling life in the alleyways is still the most fascinating thing about this particularly lively city that is full of contrasts.

TIME TRAVEL AND ISLAND BLISS
Visiting Pompeii and Herculaneum may seem like travelling back in time, but add to that the ancient imperial villa of Oplontis, another very special highlight.

1816 The Kingdom of the Two Sicilies emerges in southern Italy

1860 Naples votes to join the newly developed national state of Italy

1943 The *Quattro Giornate di Napoli*, a popular uprising in which the locals force out the fascists and Nazis occupiers

2017 The Neapolitan pizza is granted UNESCO World Heritage status

2022 In the parliamentary elections, the far-right Fratelli d'Italia becomes the strongest force with 26 per cent of the vote

Continue along the coast to Sorrento on the peninsula of the same name. Three islands lie off the Gulf of Naples that could not be more different: Capri, which – aeons ago – split from the limestone cliffs of Punta Campanella, is one of the world's most exclusive travel hotspots. Ischia and the small island of Procida are of volcanic origin. All three offer unique experiences.

La Divina Costiera, the "Divine Coast" of Amalfi, begins on the southern side of the Sorrento Peninsula, with its enchanting villages on the cliffs, terraced lemon groves and breathtaking views of the sea. The old farm tracks high above the Costiera Amalfitana offer a panoramic view, inviting you to embark on unforgettable hiking tours. Along the coast, you will find some of the most exclusive hotels located in medieval monasteries and aristocratic palaces, as well as charming, affordable accommodation in vineyards or former fishermen's cottages.

INSIDER TIP
The ancient port city of Salerno adjoins the Amalfi Coast and has what it takes to become a new iconic destination: spectacular buildings designed by international star architects have set modern trends in the historic cityscape. Local politicians have shown remarkable vision in recent decades: public transport links work perfectly, daily life for the people of Salerno is the same as in any other modern city, and the citizens stroll proudly along their well-kept harbour promenade on Sundays.

BEAUTIFUL LANDSCAPE AND UNSPOILT NATURE
Cilento, in the very south of Campania, shows how a cultural and natural landscape, which has been recognised and protected as a UNESCO World Heritage Site, can still be combined with low-impact tourism. This idyllic region begins on the plain near ancient Paestum, with its wonderfully preserved Greek temples, and then rises to imposing mountain ranges that climb to an altitude of almost 1,900m. Inland, you will find ancient farmland and welcoming local people. You can hike in protected forests, explore mysterious caves and stay on farms surrounded by nature. On the coast, long beaches, fantastic rock formations and marvellous sandy bays will delight you. A stay in unspoilt nature is offered by campsites in olive groves and holiday resorts by the turquoise and blue crystal-clear sea – the perfect contrast to lively Naples.

The Gulf of Naples is full of historical and world-class sights, and the Mediterranean flora, the national parks and the lively cities make it a well-rounded holiday destination – topped off by the warm sunlight, the mild climate and the genuine friendliness of the local people. And the icing on the cake must be the silhouette of Mount Vesuvius in the evening light – it's simply beautiful!

GET TO KNOW NAPLES & THE AMALFI COAST

AT A GLANCE

1,004,000
residents of Naples

London: 9,000,000

8,566
residents/km^2

London: 5,640/km^2

195km
Gulf of Naples coastline (not counting the Amalfi Coast and Cilento)

Isle of Wight: 92km

117.3km^2
area of Naples

Greater London: 1,572km^2

MOST POPULAR SIGHT
POMPEII

3.65 million visitors annually

WARMEST MONTH
AUGUST 30.3°C

PIZZERIAS IN NAPLES
8,200

6 UNESCO WORLD HERITAGE SIGHTS IN CAMPANIA

Historic centre of Naples; excavations at Pompeii, Herculaneum and Villa Oplontis; Royal Palace of Caserta, Vanvitelli Aqueduct and San Leucio Complex; Amalfi Coast; Paestum, Cilento and Vallo di Diano National Park with Velia Archaeolgical Park; Santa Sofia Complex of Benevento

30
Michelin-star restaurants in the Province of Naples – more than in any other Italian province

7 BLOOD MIRACLES AND 52 SAINTS IN NAPLES

UNDERSTAND NAPLES & THE AMALFI COAST

CANZONE NAPOLETANA
Naples is a musical city – it was the metropolis of melodrama in the 18th century – and it has spawned famous singers, musicians, composers and wonderfully melodic songs (that are arguably better known than the city itself!). Thse include *O sole mio*, composed by Eduardo di Capua on tour in Russia, followed by *funiculì funiculà, Santa Lucia, Torna a Surriento, Marechiaro* and many more. The *canzone napoletana* celebrate Neapolitan life and are a great advertisement for the city.

Today Naples' vibrant musical heritage continues. A famous modern musician is Pino Daniele, who died in 2015. He mixed jazz, blues and pop melodies with English and Neapolitan lyrics in a unique blend that is popular all over Italy. Gigi D'Alessio and Sal Da Vinci have also enjoyed success with catchy songs, while the band Almamegretta mixes old *tammurriata* rhythms with dub and reggae and Neapolitan dialect lyrics. There is also the so-called *neomelodici*, where the lyrics are in the Neapolitan dialect and the sound is a mix of electronic, rap and folk music. The musicians are particularly popular with urban working-class Neapolitans who celebrate them as local pop stars. Pino Daniele's rich musical legacy is continued by the band La Maschera, with its frontman Roberto Colella and their meltingly dulcet songs. Jazz fans in Naples will be blown away by the Riccardo Biseo Sanjust Quartet and their jazz interpretations of *O sole mio* and other Neapolitan classics.

BLACK PASSION
Many believe that the word *espresso* – a small cup of strong coffee – is typically Italian, but the Italians actually call it simply *caffè*. They drink it at the counters of the many standing bars found on the street corners and squares, and many are hooked on the stuff. A *caffè* early morning is usually followed by a few more over the course of the day. Italian coffee is considered among the best in the world, but in Naples *caffè* has reached perfection: full bodied yet smooth, strong

GET TO KNOW NAPLES & THE AMALFI COAST

yet aromatic and neither bitter nor acidic. This has less to do with good-quality coffee beans and more to do with the skill of the *barista* who operates the espresso machine. It is their task to adjust the grind of the bean, to prepare the ground coffee and to then apply just the right amount of pressure for the ideal amount of steam to produce the perfect cup. Neapolitans also believe that the quality of their coffee has something to do with the quality of their water.

There are countless variations: with and without sugar, *macchiato* (with a splash of frothed milk), *corretto* (with a shot of liqueur or grappa), *caffèlatte* (milk and double *caffè* in equal parts with frothed milk), *con latte* (with milk), *orzo* (barley), *freddo* (frozen), *ristretto* (more concentrated because less water is used), *doppio* (double the amount), *americano* (diluted with hot water). Unique to Naples is the old tradition of *caffè sospeso* (coffee in suspense), where a customer orders one *caffè* but pays for two. This means that a person who is down on their luck can come in and enjoy a coffee courtesy of a kind benefactor; it's a human right in Naples.

CRIMINAL CLANS

If you buy brand knock-offs from the street markets in Naples, then you will also be supporting the Camorra and organised crime. Apart from pirated products, their big business, where they make vast sums of money, consists of drugs, weapons and waste management, as well as extortion and blackmail – and, of course, construction. The organisation is made up of family clans that operate independently of one another. Over the last 20 years, the Camorra has been held responsible for more than 350 murders in Naples and the Campania region. Besides the large number of victims, the leniency programme has

Give something back with a *caffè sospeso,* for example at Naples' Gran Caffè Gambrinus

The pious and the sanctimonious: saints are everywhere in Naples

also led to successful arrests of clan members. But as long as more than half of the 900,000 unemployed in Campania are young people who see little chance of opportunities for themselves in the normal way, the Camorra will continue to find new recruits.

Alongside government efforts to fight organised crime, the anti-Mafia organisation *Libera (libera.it)* has also been active since 1995. It runs a store called *Bottega dei Sapori e dei Saperi* ("shop of good taste and good conscience") in Via Raffaele de Cesare 22, Naples, where it sells products grown organically by cooperatives on Camorra estate land which has been seized by the state.

THE CULT OF THE SAINTS

As you take your first walk through Naples, you will immediately notice that on every street corner and in almost every alleyway there is a wall shrine with a Madonna statue or saint behind glass or bars, illuminated by small lamps and decorated with artificial and fresh flowers. The poorer the area, the more lovingly maintained the shrines, and their festive lights are often in stark contrast to the peeling and smog-grimed walls surrounding them. In Naples they pay homage to 52 different saints, seven of which are particularly important, and at the top is ▶ San Gennaro, the patron saint of Naples. Three times a year, the faithful gather to witness the liquefaction of a sample of his blood in an ampoule, which takes place after fervent prayer. The Church won't allow scientists to analyse the blood, although the phenomenon has been researched. A replication study by the University of Naples in 2010 revealed that the blood was indeed from a human being. However, the way in which it liquefies remains a mystery. Shaking and rubbing the ampoules doesn't always seem to work. Anyway, religious Neapolitans are not interested in the science; they are content to believe in the miracle ... Not only does the ceremony reveal how people here seek refuge in miracles, its roots can surely be traced back to their Greek and Roman ancestors and their many pagan gods.

WASTE MANAGEMENT

Naples and its waste – still a hot topic, although some things have changed for the better. Waste and its disposal were (and are) an immensely profitable business for the Camorra.

GET TO KNOW NAPLES & THE AMALFI COAST

According to Legambiente (the Italian environmental organisation), the Camorra clans turn a 20 billion euro annual profit through waste removal, about 20 times as much as, for example, the Benetton fashion group. The city's mayors have launched waste separation programmes and called for a show of civil courage in the fight against the "waste Mafia". However, the problem is not primarily the waste produced by locals but rather the fact that the Camorra has dumped toxic waste from Italy's north into Naples' landfills and continues to do so. *Terra dei Fuochi*, the Land of Fire, is an area between Naples and Caserta which has been used as an illegal dumping ground by the rubbish Mafia for decades, and is where waste is often illegally incinerated.

NATIVITY SCENES

In Naples, Christmas nativity scenes are everywhere and go beyond the usual manger scene to contemporary or humorous tableaux, featuring everything from card-playing to fish and vegetable vendors. Children and dogs scuffle and you find camels, chickens, mice, and even lizards. All of this takes place in front of a backdrop of houses, ancient ruins, cliffs under a blue sky with clouds and beautiful angels. You have to really hunt around to find what the occasion is actually about: Mary, Joseph and baby Jesus in the manger. This art form really exploded under the Bourbon King Charles III, when each church and each family wanted their own nativity scene, and what was intended as a

TRUE OR FALSE?

SEE NAPLES & DIE

No, that's not true. The Camorra has no interest in tourists, and professional thieves are as active in Naples as they are in any other city. Of course, disreputable neighbourhoods are to be avoided late at night, but Naples is no more dangerous than other big cities.

AT LEAST THREE COURSES

Antipasto, primo, secondo, then *dolce* and a digestif: a meal like this is rarely served in everyday life. As a rule, Neapolitans eat a sandwich or a pasta dish for lunch, and a *secondo* – a main course of fish or meat – for dinner. However, on Sundays and at family celebrations Neapolitans follow the custom of eating for hours.

HIGHWAY CODE IN NEAPOLITAN

The following applies on the roads in and around Naples. Rule no.1: the biggest car has right of way. Rule no.2: if there is no free parking space, park in a second row or, if there is no other option, in a third row – or carefully drive up the stairs a few steps. Rule no.3: it is not advisable to have more than four people riding on a Vespa!

Ox, donkey, baby Jesus? How dull! Naples' nativity scene-makers have much more to offer

pious undertaking on the theme of Christ's birth grew instead into what has been described as "a collective madness". Hundreds of artisans worked throughout the year making figures and parts for the scenes; some were responsible for the vegetables, others for the animals. Great artists such as Giuseppe Sammartino and Domenico Vaccaro created wonderful figures. You can admire some of their creations in the San Martino Museum. The nativity art can be seen as a visual expression of the love of life that characterises Neapolitans. The best place to find the widest selection of nativity pieces today is in Via San Gregorio Armeno in Naples' historic centre, where it is Christmas all year round.

HOTSPOT NAPOLI

Naples has been a popular holiday destination since ancient times: the Romans thought it was chic to spend the summer in their own villas on the gulf. In the 18th century, the city by Mount Vesuvius was the final stage of the "Grand Tour", the great educational journey of the European bourgeoisie. In the 19th century, travellers from all over Europe stayed an average of three days to visit the area. Vesuvius, Paestum, Capri and Ischia beckoned. Now, with an expanded airport and a sea of B&Bs, Naples has become one of Italy's most popular holiday destinations.

The city is also experiencing a real hype in literature, with two Neapolitan authors in particular – Elena Ferrante and Roberto Saviano – recently triggering an international reading frenzy. Ferrante's novel trilogy *(My Brilliant Friend)* tells the story of a special friendship between two women from Naples in the post-war decades. There are even tours of the historic centre in the footsteps of the two heroines, with, for example *Associazione Nartea (tel. 33 97 02 08 49 | nartea.com)*. Roberto Saviano's novels *(Gomorrah, Piranhas, Savage Kiss)* provide deep insights into the everyday lives of young people in the Camorra youth clans, which are as greedy for money as they are cold-blooded.

LOTTERY? IT'S A SCIENCE

The Neapolitans all seem to believe in the power of fate and are fanatical lottery players. Figuring out how best to predict the winning numbers has produced a veritable industry of lottery oracles and advisers, as well as "counsellors" who interpret dreams, events and experiences and then convert them into numbers. These lists of numbers are called ▶ *smorfie*, a term that comes from Morpheus, the god of sleep and dreams. In the historic centre of Naples, the lottery offices and bookmakers have plenty of *smorfie* books, a particularly Neapolitan curiosity. The documentary *Dreaming by Numbers* offers some fascinating insights into this elaborate system of choosing lottery numbers.

SLOW FOOD IN CAMPANIA

The Italians call it *chilometro zero* when food is grown or produced in the region where it's consumed. These "zero kilometre" products are the basis of slow-food cuisine. The international Slow Food movement was founded in Italy in 1986, and is especially evident in Campania. It strives to preserve and promote traditional regional cuisine using local foods produced by local businesses. Biodiversity, diversity of culinary cultures, fair conditions for producers and the enjoyment of the consumer are the movement's focus.

Campania Slow Food products include the typical ▶ *alici di menaica*, anchovies that are caught using ancient methods by the fishermen in Pisciotta and preserved in brine. Other taste ambassadors of the movement are white artichokes from Pertosa, beans from Controne, the Piennolo del Vesuvio tomato variety or the famous Pomodoro San Marzano (the best tinned tomatoes). The slow-food guru from Campania, Luciano Pignataro, posts restaurant tips on his blog *lucianopignataro.it*. The Slow Food movement inspired the *città slow* movement, governed by a philosophy of sustainability and improved quality of life in towns. In Campania, towns such as Amalfi, Pollica, Positano and Paestum are part of its network. *slowfood.it/campania, cittaslow.org*

EATING SHOPPING SPORT

Amalfi's picturesque beach

EATING & DRINKING

Campania is probably the lushest region in Italy. On the outskirts of Naples, the green *campania felix* (happy country) has carefully cultivated fields with rich, dark volcanic soil, where countless varieties grow year round: artichokes, broccoli, *cime de rapa* (a kale variety), the typically Campanian *friarielli* (a slightly peppery leaf), young green asparagus, peppers, aubergines, courgettes and every type of salad leaf and cabbage.

IN THE LAND OF THE "LEAF EATERS"

The Neapolitans already had a penchant for green vegetables in the 18th century, which is why they were popularly known as *mangiafogli*, leaf eaters. Vegetables are marinated in oil, stuffed, grilled and flavoured with lemon, garlic and *peperoncino* (chilli), but pasta is also dressed with vegetables in all kinds of variations.

THE FAMOUS TOMATO

Everywhere there are tomatoes: the large, bright red meaty tomatoes from Sorrento, ideal as a salad and in the *caprese*, then the small, sweet cherry tomatoes, the *pomodorini del piennolo*, which thrive in the fertile soil around Mount Vesuvius, and are sun-dried in bundles then used as a pizza base, on *bruschetta* and in tomato stock.

However, the most famous tomatoes from the *campania felix* are the heirloom variety of plum tomato or the *pummarola*, as the Neapolitans say, the *San Marzano*, from which the *sugo* is prepared. *Sugo* is added to all the varieties of pasta. The sugo sauce is also used for cooking fish and meat, and you simply can't have an authentic Neapolitan pizza without the tomato sauce as its base. Olives, capers, oregano, garlic, *peperoncino* and basil are the seasonings.

So sweet, so crispy: a morning without *sfogliatelle* (right) is unthinkable!

A STARRING ROLE FOR PASTA

In addition to tomatoes, pasta also plays a crucial role. The traditional local varieties include *maccheroni della zita* (thick, long spaghetti), the thick and long *scialatielli*, often made by hand, and the short, broad tube noodles from Gragnano called *paccheri*. Then, of course, there's spaghetti and *linguine*, the flat, long strings of pasta.

The most delicious pasta dishes come from the poor man's kitchen: *pasta alla puttanesca*, *pasta alla genovese* or *pasta e fagioli* and *pasta e patate* respectively: all are made from leftovers or inexpensive ingredients. The queen of Neapolitan pasta dishes is *pasta al ragù*: pasta in a particularly intense tomato sauce because the Sunday roast has been simmering in it for hours. Traditionally, this *primo* is served on Sundays before the main course.

BUT WHAT ABOUT PIZZA?

Pizza is the pride and joy of Neapolitans. They would be lost without their signature dish. But what's the secret to a good pizza? The dough must be rolled out to be round and almost wafer-thin in the centre but leaving its edges bulging. And the ingredients must be fresh. The classic is the pizza margherita, a base of tomato sauce topped with buffalo mozzarella (or the cow's milk variety, *fior di latte*) and basil leaves – *basta*! *Margherita a filetto* is the alternative made with fresh tomatoes. Last, but not least, the combination of tomato sauce with garlic and oregano is known as a *marinara*. All other concoctions are a no-go, especially for purists, and some pizzerias only sell these three types.

Pizza is the ubiquitous street food, and a slice to go is the perfect snack for in between meals. It all came about in the early 19th century, when bakers would bake the leftovers of dough, which boys would then sell the next day on the street from trays hanging around their necks. Somebody then had the brainwave of filling the bread with vegetables or fried fish leftovers or even just a slug of olive oil and a sprinkling of salt – and the pizza was born.

THE SEA ON YOUR DOORSTEP

Campania also has many seafood and fish dishes, including anchovies *(alici)*, red mullet *(triglia)*, scorpion fish *(scorfano)*, red bream *(cernia)*, sea bass *(orata)*, sole *(sogliola)*, swordfish *(pesce spada)*, mackerel *(sgombro)*, squid (*calamaro, seppia*), octopus *(polipo)*, but especially mussels *(cozze)* and the favourite clams *(vongole veraci)*. A real Slow Food delicacy are the anchovies from Cetara, on the Amalfi Coast *(alici cetaresi)*, and from Pisciotta on the coast of Cilento.

> **INSIDER TIP**
> A slow food delicacy

Besides pork *(maiale)* and beef *(manzo)*, kid goat *(capretto)* is a popular dish in Cilento, while lamb *(agnello)* and rabbit *(coniglio)* are popular on Ischia. Buffalo meat is also growing in popularity.

CHEESE OR PUDDING? BOTH!

Sweets, pastries and desserts also have a long tradition in Campania: ▪ *sfogliatelle*, dumplings made from puff pastry or shortcrust pastry, are available in every *pasticceria*. *Babà*, a sweet yeast dough cake soaked in rum, and Sicilian *cannoli*, deep-fried dough rolls filled with ricotta, are also popular. Important ingredients are candied fruits and *ricotta*, the light fresh cheese made from the whey of cow or sheep's milk.

There are also some excellent cheeses in Campania. The king of the local cheeses has to be the buffalo milk mozzarella *(di bufala)*, light, moist and creamy – nothing at all like the rubbery mozzarella in our supermarkets. Other fresh cheeses are *scamorza*, which you can have either smoked or grilled, and the pale yellow *provolone*.

Naturally, Campania also produces its own wines. The vines on the slopes of Mount Vesuvius produce both red and white wines, which carry the *Lacryma Christi* label. Excellent Campania white wines (with Italy's top classification, DOCG) are *Fiano di Avellino* and *Greco di Tufo,* or the *Biancolella* from Ischia. Full-bodied, award-winning Campania red wines are *Taurasi* and *Aglianico del Taburno*. The wines from Cilento have also stepped up to the mark in the annual *Vini d'Italia* wine tastings. This is thanks to the dedication of vintners such as Bruno De Conciliis, Luigi Maffini, Marisa Cuomo, Francesco Barone, Ciro Macellaro and Ida Budetta, who grow characteristic indigenous varieties such as *Aglianico* (red) and *Fiano* (white). A simple yet tasty wine is the lightly sparkling *Gragnano*.

Regional liqueurs are *limoncello* or *limoncino* made from the thick skins of the ▪ Amalfi lemon, *limone sfusato*. There is also Amaro Strega, a herbal liqueur made in Benevento. If you are offered a home-made basil liqueur, it will be one of the most delicious liqueurs you have ever tasted!

EATING & DRINKING

TODAY'S SPECIALS

Antipasti

CAPRESE
Mozzarella with tomatoes and basil

ZUCCHINE ALLA SCAPECE
Fried courgette slices, cooled and served with a dash of vinegar and mint

ALICI MARINATE
Raw anchovies, marinated in lemon juice

MOZZARELLA IN CAROZZA
Crumbed, fried sandwiches, filled with mozzarella

Primi e pizze

SPAGHETTI ALLE VONGOLE
Spaghetti with small clams, garlic, olive oil and parsley

LINGUINE ALLA PUTTANESCA
Linguine with tomato sauce, olives, capers, anchovies and parsley

FUSILLI ALLA GENOVESE
Fusilli pasta with beef ragu, carrots and lots of onions

PARMIGIANA DI MELANZANE
Slices of aubergines, tomato sauce and mozzarella, sprinkled with parmesan and baked in the oven

GATTÒ DI PATATE
Savoury bake made with potatoes, egg, ham and soft cheese

CALZONE
Turnover made with pizza dough, filled with ham, mozzarella, ricotta and parmesan

Secondi

FRITTO MISTO
Fried rice balls, shrimps and chunks of fish and vegetables

FRIARIELLI IN PADELLA CON SALSICCIA
Cabbage leaves steamed in garlic and chilli with pork sausage

CODA DI ROSPO ALL'ACQUA PAZZA
Monkfish in a sauce made with oil, garlic, tomato, wine and water

IMPEPATA DI COZZE
Mussels with lemon, parsley and freshly ground black pepper

POLIPI AFFOGATI
Small octopus simmered in tomato sauce

TOTANI E PATATE
Squid and potato stew

SHOPPING

SOUVENIRS FOR CONNOISSEURS

Extend the holiday feeling by taking home local delicacies: Neapolitan *taralli*, crackers baked in pork fat with almonds, are just as much a hit as air-dried Neapolitan salami or dried or oil-packed anchovies. Other culinary treats that make good souvenirs are vegetables marinated in oil or vinegar – aubergines, courgettes, mushrooms, artichokes – the *sott'oli* or *sott'aceti*. Or opt for espresso coffee, or the excellent extra-virgin olive oil from Cilento, or the ever-present *limoncello*, the delicious lemon liqueur, especially from Capri, Sorrento and Amalfi, or even a fresh mozzarella (also lactose-free), which you can order online just before your departure at *aeroportodinapoli.it/eshop/mozzarella-gift*. It is then packed airtight for the journey and all you have to do is pick it up and pay.

> **INSIDER TIP**
> From Naples with love

BELLA NAPOLI TO TAKE HOME

The *centro storico* of Naples is a treasure trove for regional specialities: along the Spaccanapoli main street, but also in the side alleyways and courtyards, there are small shops selling leather bags, handmade soap, creative jewellery and paper items. There is even a whole street exclusively dedicated to nativity scenes, the Via San Gregorio Armeno, which transforms into a colourful bazaar at Christmas time. Here you will find the famous Neapolitan nativity figures, including contemporary personalities such as Donald Trump and Cristiano Ronaldo.

In *Napolimania* at Naples airport you can find souvenirs that play off the city's clichés: how about a little red horn, an amulet used for protection from the *malocchio*, the evil eye? The nicest of these are made by the terracotta artist *Ulderico Pinfildi (Via San Biagio dei Librai 113)*. The ultimate

Gragnano near Naples is Italy's pasta capital (right)

souvenir can be found at the shop of creative jewellery designer *Gustavo Renna (Via Domenico Morelli 53)*, for example the traditional Naples washing line styled into a necklace.

LOCAL TRADITION
In Amalfi and Tramonti, the tradition of making fine paper has survived, and the paper makes a wonderful souvenir as it is easy to transport. In Sorrento, the art of wood inlays thrives: there are boxes and chests, trays, frames and much more. Ceramic and majolica vases and crockery have been traditionally crafted on the coast (Vietri sul Mare). And at San Leucio you can purchase the most beautiful silk fabrics.

LA GRANDE BELLEZZA
Naples – southern Italy's capital of fashion – has a great selection of interesting boutiques selling local labels. They can be found in *Via Toledo* and *Corso Umberto* (for cheaper stores), and in the Chiaia quarter in the streets around *Piazza dei Martiri* (more high-end labels), as well as in *Via Scarlatti* in *Vomero* (international and expensive labels). Many boutiques on the Amalfi Coast sell casual summer fashion made from colourful, airy natural fabrics. In Positano *(Bottega di Brunella)* and on Capri *(Laboratorio Capri, Ecocapri, Farella)*, local designers offer attractive hand-crafted fashion, the Capri sandal being a typical item.

HAGGLE & BARGAIN WITH RELISH
Whether you're shopping or people-watching, the markets here are always a pleasure. Vegetables, fruit, fish, clothing and household items are sold in Naples every morning at the Antignano market in the Vomero quarter or on the Piazza Pignasecca. Fashion-lovers flock to the huge, daily second-hand market on Corso Resina in Ercolano.

SPORT & ACTIVITIES

You can work up a sweat just strolling through the streets of Positano or Capri: steep steps lead up and down through the towns. The same is true in Naples, where there are over 200 stairways; you can find four beautiful, panoramic stairways on *scaledinapoli.com* (search for *Quattro scale per cominciare*).

In the sultry heat of the south, the approach to sports is more easy-going than it is in the sports-mad north (especially in the upper Adriatic Sea near Rimini or on Lake Garda). But on the Gulf of Naples and in Cilento there are still plenty of options for the sporty and the energetic. Typical beach activities, such as beach volleyball, are possible on the wide sandy beaches of Paestum, Marina di Ascea, Marina di Camerota and Palinuro in Cilento. They are also offered at the many campsites and holiday resorts that are situated right on the beach.

The Amalfi Coast, Capri, Ischia and the wildly romantic Cilento are ideal for excursions into nature – whether on foot, by bicycle or e-bike, or on horseback. Outdoor and nature tour operators have for some time promoted this mountainous landscape (for example, *cilento-travel.com/en.html*). The tourist information bureaux and the internet provide contacts for bicycle rentals, riding stables and tour guides. For additional information about an active Cilento holiday, visit *walking-trekking.com*, which covers each section of Cilento in great detail.

CYCLING

With its well-built network of roads and quieter traffic conditions, the Cilento region is a more relaxed alternative to, say, Mallorca for keen cyclists. An excellent place to start from in Capaccio Scalo is the bicycle shop *Ciclidea (SS 18 km 90 | tel. 08 28*

If your legs hurt from hiking on Ischia, end the day with a revitalising swim

72 35 64 | *ciclidea.eu)*, where Pino Giovinal is on hand with good tips. Cycling on Procida is a very special experience: the island, which is just 4km² in size, is easily manageable. E-bikes are also available for those who prefer a less strenuous ride: it's marvellous to be able to zip across the island and explore its beaches and coves in a single day.

Naples can also be experienced by bike: a recommended hire service is *Napoli Bike (Riviera di Chiaia 201 | tel. 0 81 41 19 34 | napolibike.com)*. On the sea-facing side of the Villa Comunale park, many families cycle along the promenade, which is partially closed to traffic, especially on Sundays. While most locals prefer to stay with the crowd, you might want to discover Mergellina or Posillipo Hill. The many views are well worth the effort.

HIKING

There are plenty of beautiful hiking areas to choose from in Campania. One of these is the island of Ischia *(ischiatrekking.net)*, with its Monte Epomeo. Another area is the Monti Lattari *(parcoregionaledeimontilattari.it)* mountain range, with Monte Faito, which rises up inland from the Sorrento Peninsula. The Amalfi Coast has numerous paths (often old mule tracks) that are ideal for hiking *(cartotrekking.com)*. They may be steep and rocky in parts, but the rewards are the magnificent views from the vantage points. Finally, there is Cilento, with its pristine, mountainous landscape – as yet undiscovered by tourists – with interesting ridge walks over the Monti Alburni mountains or on Monte Cervati. Or you can hike on Monte Sacro's devotional trails (it is also known as Monte Gelbison) to the important Madonna sanctuary.

As a general rule, it is essential to stay on the trails! Due to the partly exposed coastal paths and the volcanic subsoil, accidents can occur when reckless hikers leave the trails. Depending on your plans, local hiking guides are advisable – and quite affordable. The tourist offices provide help with route maps and addresses of hiking organisations. Good websites with hiking routes, tips and contacts are *amalficoastrekking.com/en/list-of-hikes.html, cartotrekking.com, giovis.com* and *everytrail.com* (search under Campania) and on *Instagram: caprihiking*.

HORSE RIDING

In Cilento, you can experience wonderful rides along the beaches, in the Mediterranean maquis, and in the lush forests of the nature reserve, on the high plateaux of the Vallo di Diano or through the Mingardo and Calore river valleys. For information on riding stables visit, for example, *www.agriturismoimoresani.com/en/activities/riding-holidays*

KAYAKING

When you tire of the sea and the beach and want to experience fresh, cool water in a wild, romantic, mountainous setting, then a great option is to go kayaking through the Calore ravines and gorges near Felitto *(goledelcalore.it)*. Kayaking and rafting trips are also available on the Sele or Tanagro rivers *(campobase.org, tpescursioni.it)*. For a different view of the coast, try kayaking on the Amalfitana *(amalfikayak.com)*, in Cilento *(italykayaktours.com)* and in Naples *(kayaknapoli.com)*. These tours show Naples from the sea and take you along the picturesque coast of Posillipo.

PARAGLIDING

A top spot for hang-gliders and paragliders is only a short drive from the ancient temples of Paestum on the slopes of Monte Soprano. During the day, a strong updraft develops with south/southwesterly winds. A few minutes after take-off you can reach heights of 700m. Starting and landing spots can be seen at *yumping.it*.

SCUBA DIVING

The sea around Campania's coast and its islands is a diver's paradise, and there are numerous dive schools in the resorts that supply dive equipment and offer courses and diving trips. The Sorrento Peninsula offers some great diving opportunities, including the Punta Campanella's Parco Marino and off the rocky cliffs of the Punta del Capo. In addition to the marine creatures and a rich underwater flora, there is also a Madonna figure dedicated to seafarers in the diving grounds at the Massa Lubrense harbour. The underground grottos such as the Grotta dello Zaffiro at Punta Campanella, on the tip of the Sorrento Peninsula, are very impressive. A recommended operator is *Diving Nettuno (Villaggio Nettuno | Marina del Cantone | tel. 08 18 08 10 51 | divingsorrento. com)*.

You can dive everywhere along the Amalfi Coast; one dive centre follows

SPORT & ACTIVITIES

the next. The beautiful Cilento coastline is perforated by grottos and full of coves and bays, making it ideal for divers. In Palinuro, one of many dive centres is the *Palinuro Sub Diving Center | Via Porto | tel. 3 36 70 66 71 | palinurosub.it.*

A very special experience is the diving in the underwater Archaeology Park of 🕆 Baia, near Naples: you dive among the remains of the once-magnificent ancient Roman summer villas, with, for example, *Centro Sub Campi Flegrei (Via Miliscola 165 | Pozzuoli | tel. 08 18 53 15 63 | centrosubcampiflegrei.it).*

WINDSURFING & SAILING

Classic water-sport activities such as sailing, stand-up paddleboarding, surfing and kite-surfing are offered all along the coast. Good surfing conditions can be found at Paestum, Agropoli, Marina di Casal Velino and Palinuro. A real hotspot is Cetara, where you can also book individual sessions (in advance) at *windsurfingcetara.com*.

YOGA

A very special version of yoga comes from Naples, where Valeria Barbaro has founded *Yoga Fly on Air (tel. 33 56 55 84 40 | yogaflyonair.com)*:

> **INSIDER TIP**
> **Lift off and switch off**

you look like a bat when you are suspended in a kind of hammock at *Galleria Umberto I* and practise the *asanas* in the air, defying gravity.

Campania is one of Italy's top diving regions

REGIONAL OVERVIEW

NAPLES p. 38

HERCULANEUM & POMPEII p. 58

CAPRI, ISCHIA, PROCIDA p. 72

SORRENTO & THE AMALFI COAST p. 84

Trio of islands with spectacular nature and their own unique flair

- Volturno
- Caserta
- Aversa
- Acerra
- Giugliano in Campania
- Casoria
- Nola
- **NAPOLI**
- Pozzuoli
- Procida
- Torre Annunziata
- Pagani
- Nocera
- Ischia
- Golfo di Napoli
- Castellammare
- Cava
- Salerno
- Sorrento
- Capri

Mare Tirreno

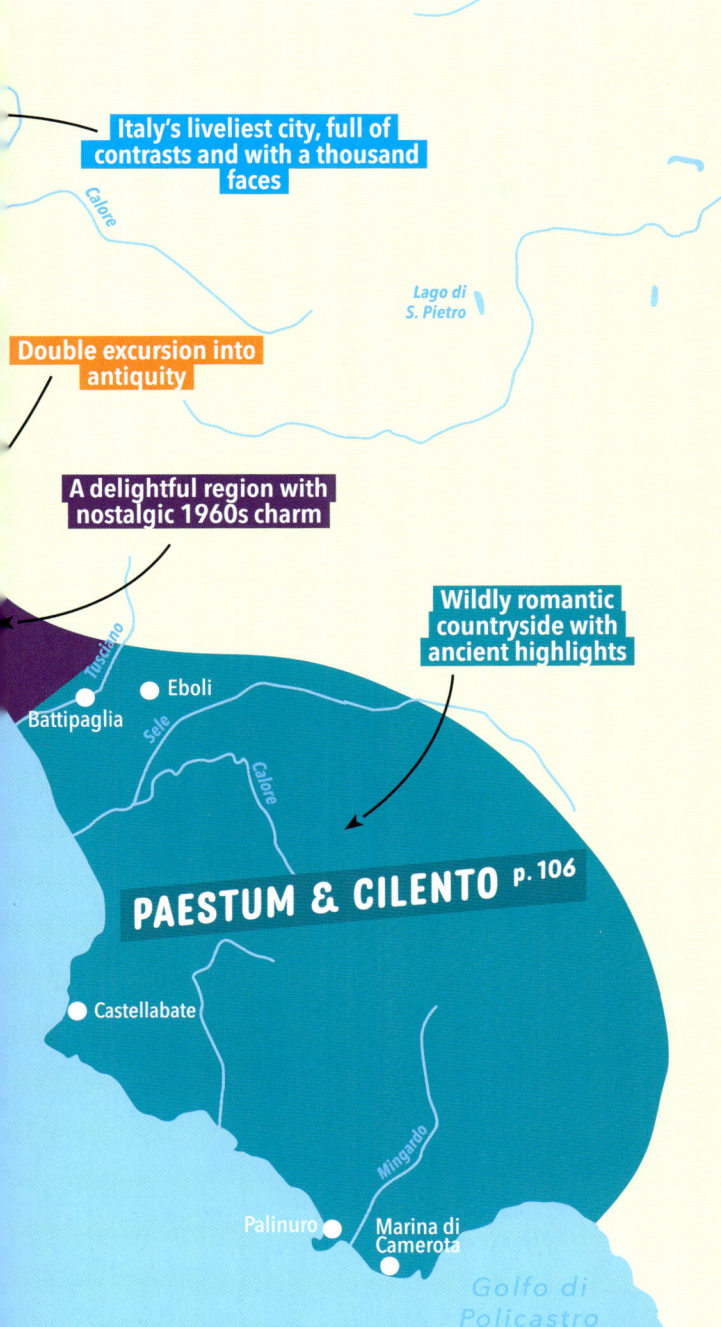

NAPLES

THRILLING & BEAUTIFUL

You may be a little nervous before your visit to the city of Naples. Will you find your way around in the densely populated old town? Is traffic really as crazy and chaotic as they claim?

It is always advisable to be cautious, yet Naples is no more frenetic or dangerous than other major European cities. The Camorra – like other Mafia gangs in (southern) Italy – still plays a big role, but its presence goes unnoticed by tourists. And, despite the gritty chaos and grime, there is also the warm friendliness of the locals, hearty

Peeling plaster and lots of improvisation, but fruit and vegetables are always first class!

laughter, leafy squares, the radiant blue of sky and sea, and the aroma of *caffè*, sweet pastries and pizza.

Naples also has a modern side, with glass and steel skyscrapers by Kenzo Tanges in the east of the city and the award-winning art stations on Metro Lines 1 and 6. And the people of Naples have transformed their historic centre into a wonderful open-air museum with street art called *murales*.

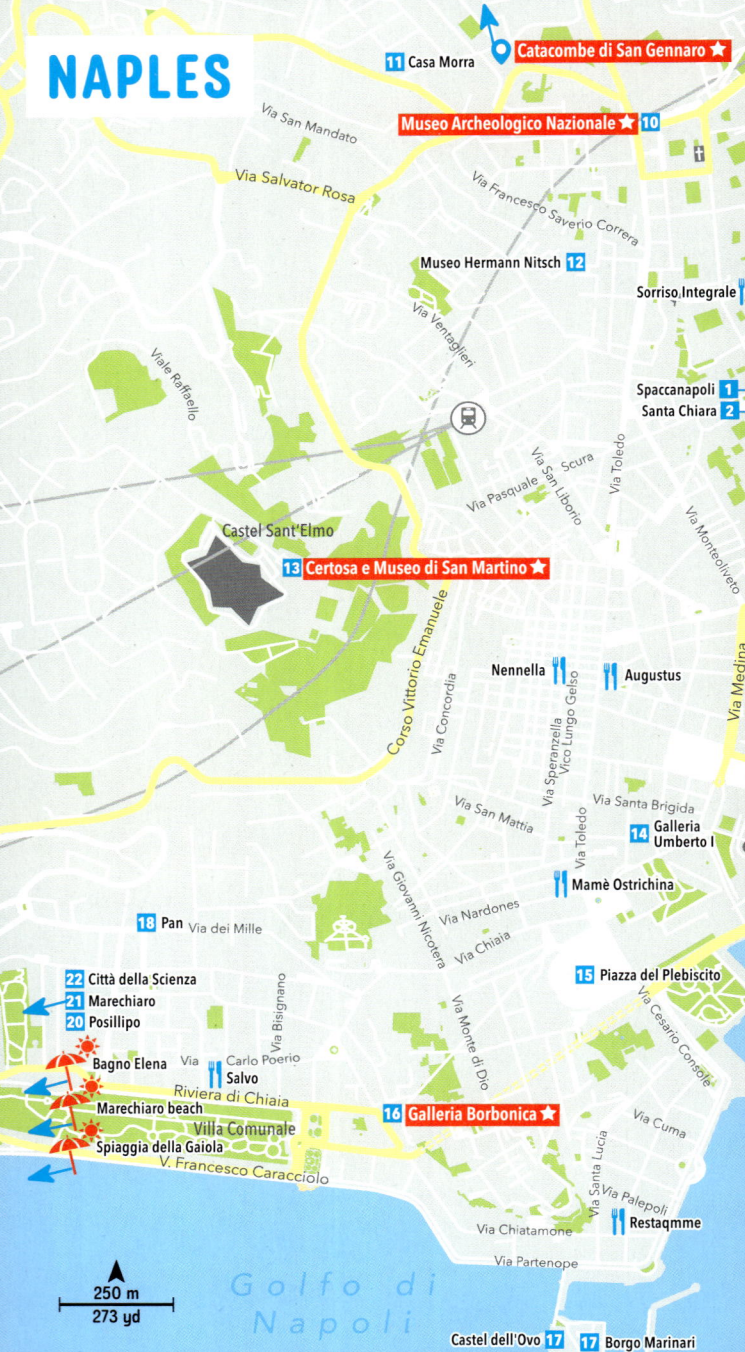

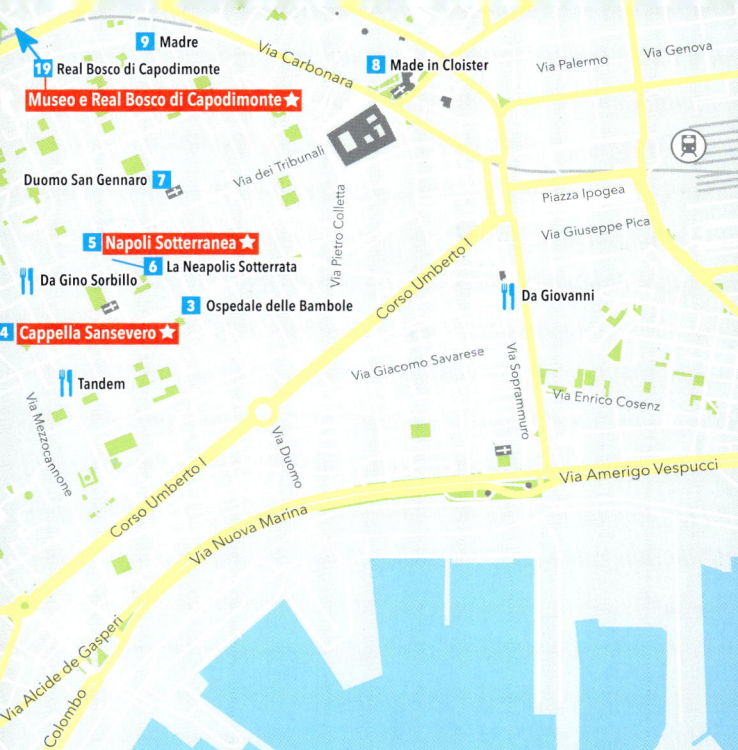

MARCO POLO HIGHLIGHTS

★ CAPPELLA SANSEVERO
The private chapel of the Prince of Sansevero is stunningly beautiful ➤ p. 44

★ NAPOLI SOTTERRANEA
Suspense in Naples' underworld: discover wartime bunkers and Camorra hideouts ➤ p. 44

★ MUSEO ARCHEOLOGICO NAZIONALE
The most magnificent mosaics and paintings from Pompeii, as well as the secret cabinet of erotic art, entice visitors ➤ p. 46

★ CERTOSA E MUSEO DI SAN MARTINO
Naples in miniature: the cloister's collection of nativity scenes, as well as the best ever belvedere ➤ p. 47

★ GALLERIA BORBONICA
Once an escape route for the Neapolitan king, now an adventure playground for adults ➤ p. 47

★ MUSEO E REAL BOSCO DI CAPODIMONTE
The rich art collection is considered to be the "Louvre at Vesuvius" ➤ p. 48

★ STAZIONI DELL'ARTE
The art stations on Metro Line 1 are like the coolest of art galleries ➤ p. 49

★ CATACOMBE DI SAN GENNARO
Travel back in time 2,000 years and explore the secret tombs of the early Christians ➤ p. 50

★ CUMA
Once home to the famous Greek oracle Sibyl ➤ p. 57

Napoli, **capital city of the Campania region, is Italy's third largest city.** With one million inhabitants, its population density is four times greater than that of Rome, but the population swells to three million when the sprawling metropolitan area outside the city limits is included. There are some 300 churches, numerous palaces, castles and monasteries tucked away within the city. Naples is more popular than ever before: the number of visitors has more than doubled since 2010, new hotels and, especially, B&Bs are booming, and the city is the setting for crime thrillers and films.

Each era, each regime, has left behind its insignia: medieval fortresses and Gothic churches, that were given a facelift by the splendorous Baroque of the Counter-Reformation. In the 18th century, when Naples was one of Europe's most magnificent and important cities, the "good" King Charles commissioned the sumptuous San Carlo Theatre, the grand royal palaces of Capodimonte, Caserta and Portici and, last but not least, the massive Albergo dei Poveri (Hostel for the Poor).

The best way to explore the confined, traffic-calmed city centre – with its sightseeing attractions tucked away in a maze of alleyways – is on foot. Due to the location of the attractions, this guide does not indicate the transport links. Buses (C57, R2, R4) travel along the arterial roads that flank the old town and the cable railway connects the city's high-lying districts.

The long, straight *Spaccanapoli* splits the *centro storico* in two parts (*spaccare* means to split). Another important landmark is *Via Toledo*, a grand boulevard during the time of the Spanish viceroys and today one of the city's main shopping streets: from the former Reggia Capodimonte (here still called Corso Amedeo di Savoia) it leads down towards the sea and flanks the chaotic district of *Sanità* to the left, *Quartieri Spagnoli* to the right. Then Via Toledo touches the historic old town at Piazza Dante and reaches the Palazzo Reale at Piazza del Plebiscito at its end.

The *Santa Lucia* neighbourhood is by the sea; from the coastal roads Via Nazario Sauro and Via Partenope the large, luxurious traditional hotels look out on to the rock fortification of the Castel dell'Ovo. In the north and west of the city, is the wide open area of *"Napoli bene"*, the upper middle-class *Chiaia San Ferdinando* with stately properties and a few nice hotels, fine shops, the elegant Piazza dei Martiri and many trendy restaurants, or the more anonymous district of *Vomero* which lies higher up, with its popular

WHERE TO START?

From the **Piazza Trieste e Trento** *(*⌶⌶ *f5)* it is easy to explore on foot in all directions: to the Piazza del Plebiscito next door, shopping in the Chiaia quarter or through the Via Toledo pedestrian zone to the *centro storico* in 30 minutes. Get there by bus R2 from the main station or by Metro Line 1, Municipio stop.

NAPLES

Street art metropolis Napoli even features patron saint Gennaro

Piazza Vanvitelli, and the wonderful *Posillipo,* whose villas overlook the sea.

SIGHTSEEING

1 SPACCANAPOLI

The most famous street in downtown Naples, Spaccanapoli or "split Naples", is officially not one street at all but the nickname given to a sequence of streets (namely Via Domenico Capitelli, Via Benedetto Croce and Via San Biagio dei Librai) that cut through the heart of the historic centre. The Spaccanapoli is like an open-air museum: take a look into its lanes and palace courtyards, into the churches and chapels and its shops and ateliers. Along the way, the façades are adorned with ancient Roman marble elements, and the tiny altars of saints on the street corners are part of Naples' cultural history. In 1995, the old town was awarded UNESCO World Heritage status. In terms of its architecture, nothing may be altered but this doesn't stop the street from changing its cultural make-up. Walk into the aristocratic *Palazzo Marigliano* and you'll discover a printing shop just as it was in olden times; the famous dolls' museum *Ospedale delle Bambole*; the well-known publishers Editoriale Scientifica; and a workshop making nativity scenes. *f-g3*

2 SANTA CHIARA

All the superlatives you can think of spring to mind when you see this church: Santa Chiara is Naples' largest convent basilica, built in French Gothic style. The medieval tomb of Robert of Anjou, known as Robert the Wise, is the largest of the many royal tombs inside the church. The cloister courtyard, *Chiostro delle Clarisse,* is an impressive space, made pretty by the nuns with majolica-tiled benches and fragrant lemon and orange trees everywhere. The entrance to the cloister leads to the room with the massive nativity scene from the 18th/19th century. *Mon–Sat 9.30am–5.30pm, Sun 10am–2.30pm | Via Benedetto Croce/Via Santa Chiara 49c | monastero disantachiara.it | ⊙ 1 hr | ⌸ f–g3*

3 OSPEDALE DELLE BAMBOLE 👫

This doll and toy paradise is a pure delight for the young and the young at heart: Dottoressa Tiziana Grassi and her family have been repairing dolls from around the world in her dolls' hospital at Palazzo Marigliano for over 100 years. *Mon, Thu–Sat 10.30am–1.30pm and 3.30–6.30pm, Sun 10am–1.30pm, booking recommended | Via San Biagio dei Librai 39 | ospedaledellebambole.com | ⊙ 1 hr. | ⌸ g3*

4 CAPPELLA SANSEVERO ★

A place of pilgrimage for visitors from around the world who come to see the sculpture of Christ with its marble veil, dating back to 1753. Legend has it that the veil was melted into the marble statue, created by the sculptor Giuseppe Sammartino, by means of the art of alchemy. The "magic potion" was reputedly the invention of Raimondo di Sangro, Prince of Sansevero, who has gone down in history as a famous inventor and alchemist. *Wed–Mon 9am–7pm | Via Francesco De Sanctis 19–21 | museosansevero.it | ⌸ g3*

5 NAPOLI SOTTERRANEA (NAPLES UNDERGROUND) ★ 🚩

Naples Underground is not for the claustrophobic: 42m beneath the ground, this unique labyrinth is a maze of tunnels, cisterns and sewage systems, which were cut into the soft volcanic lava by the Greeks and Romans. The tunnels were used until the late 19th century as an aqueduct system and later as a dumping ground for waste, as well as air-raid shelters during World War II. Top of the must-see list! *Daily 10am–6pm every hour on the hour, guided tours in English 10am, noon, 2pm, 4pm, 6pm | Piazza San Gaetano 68 | napolisotterranea. org | ⊙ 2 hrs | ⌸ g2*

6 LA NEAPOLIS SOTTERRATA 🌂

The excavations under the Gothic monastery church of *San Lorenzo Maggiore* are unique: in the 20th century, one of the monks discovered traces of ancient buildings. Today, a well-preserved Roman shopping street with a bakery, wine bar and the remains of a marketplace can be seen two storeys below ground. *Daily 9.30am–5.30pm | Piazza San Gaetano 316 | laneapolissotterrata.it | ⊙ 1 hr | ⌸ g2*

7 DUOMO SAN GENNARO

Miracles are by definition unpredictable and spontaneous, except in this Gothic cathedral. By appointment, three times a year, 🚩 San Gennaro miraculously liquefies his own blood in front of the praying Neapolitan congregation. If all goes well, his dry blood, which is kept stored in

NAPLES

The mesmerising dome frescoes in San Gennaro are as busy as a *Where's Wally* picture!

ampoules, will turn into liquid on 19 September, 12 December and on the Saturday before the first Sunday in May. If it doesn't, the fear is that the city will witness a disaster. However, if the city's patron saint is merciful and keeps his appointment for liquefaction, locals will take to the streets in celebration, especially in May and September. San Gennaro's ampoule of blood is treasured in a side chapel *(Mon–Sat 8.30am–1pm and 2.30–7.30pm, Sun 8am–1pm and 4.30–7.30pm, avoid visiting on Sun am, reduced visiting hours in Aug)*.

The *cathedral museum (daily 9.30am–6.30pm | museosangennaro.it)* next door is also interesting for its collection of Saint Gennaro's jewels, which are said to be worth more than the Crown Jewels of the United Kingdom! *Via Duomo 149 | g–h2*

8 MADE IN CLOISTER

Thanks to its morbid charm, this former Renaissance monastery has developed into a cool cultural temple with exciting exhibitions and concerts usually only announced at short notice. *Wed–Sat 11am–7pm | Piazza Enrico de Nicola 46 | madeincloister.com | h2*

9 MADRE

Internationally acclaimed temporary exhibitions at the *Museo d'Arte Contemporanea Donnaregina*, the young museum in the historic centre, whet the appetite for contemporary art. The museum's exciting permanent collection, which is to be expanded into the art archive of Campania, includes some of the best international artists of the last 50 years: Joseph Beuys, Andy Warhol, Richard Serra, Jeff Koons, Jannis Kounellis and Mimmo Paladino, who also create(d)

Shop in style at the elegant Galleria Umberto I

works of art in Naples. *Mon and Wed–Sat 10am–7.30pm, Sun 10am–8pm | Via Settembrini 79 | madrenapoli.it | ⓘ 2 hrs | ⏵ g1*

10 MUSEO ARCHEOLOGICO NAZIONALE ★

Naples' National Archaeological Museum exhibits most of the Roman artefacts excavated in Pompeii, Herculaneum and elsewhere in the Gulf of Naples since the mid-18th century. The museum was established by the Bourbon king Charles VII, who wanted to show off his exquisite collection of unique artefacts, ranging from Roman sculptures, mosaics and frescoes to delicate landscape and portrait paintings from Pompeii villas. The *Gabinetto Segreto* offers a different theme altogether: once reserved for men of the Royal Court, this "secret chamber" contains a collection of ancient erotica from the brothels of Pompeii and sex toys of the rich Romans (minimum age for admission: 12 years). It's extraordinary to think that nothing much has changed in 2,000 years! *Wed–Mon 9am–7.30pm | Piazza Museo | mann-napoli.it | ⓘ 2½ hrs | ⏵ f2*

11 CASA MORRA

Contemporary art in a noble mansion setting: the patron Giuseppe Morra has planned a series of alternating shows for the next 100 years of his ambitious exhibition project. His aim is to rejuvenate the run-down neighbourhood of Materdei. *Tue–Fri 10am–6pm, Sat 10am–2pm | Salita San Raffaele 20c | Metro 1 Materdei | fondazionemorra.org | ⏵ e2*

**INSIDER TIP
100 years of art**

12 MUSEO HERMANN NITSCH

In the small streets above Piazza Dante, art patron Giuseppe Morra pays homage to Austrian avant-garde artist Hermann Nitsch in a converted power

NAPLES

station. Blood is omnipresent in Nitsch's so-called "action painting". If the documentation of the artist's orgies with blood and guts is too much for you, you can relax on the terrace with a marvellous view over Naples. Sept–July Mon–Fri 10am–7pm, Sat/Sun 10am–4pm | Vico Lungo Pontecorvo 29d | museonitsch.org | ○ 1 hr | ▥ f3

13 CERTOSA E MUSEO DI SAN MARTINO ★

The beautiful gardens, the traditional Neapolitan nativities in the museum and the delightful views of the Gulf of Naples are all great reasons to visit this imposing Carthusian monastery. The breathtaking view over the vast sea of houses below is the highlight. Towering in the background to the far east of the Vomero plateau is the fortress *Castel Sant'Elmo (daily 8.30am–7.30pm)* with its interesting exhibitions of contemporary art. *Wed–Mon 8.30am–7.30pm | Largo San Martino | short.travel/golf9 | Funicolare Montesanto* | ○ 1½ hrs | ▥ e4

14 GALLERIA UMBERTO I

Milan already had one, so Naples simply had to follow suit and build this replica of Milan's Galleria Vittorio Emanuele II. Covered with a vast glass dome, the elegant shopping arcade is similar in style to many other arcades built in Europe at the end of the 19th century. Take the lift up to the fourth floor, visit the *Art Resort* hotel and see Naples from a different perspective!

Somewhat hidden away opposite the entrance to the Teatro San Carlo is *Ascione (Mon 4.30–7.30pm, Tue–Sat 10.30am–1.30pm and 4.30–7.30pm, please ring the bell | ascione.it),* which exhibits sensational pieces of jewellery from a historic coral processor and jeweller (open since 1855!). *Via Toledo/Via San Carlo* | ▥ f5

INSIDER TIP Admire the red gold

15 PIAZZA DEL PLEBISCITO

Every Sunday, the grand neoclassical *Piazza del Plebiscito* turns into a hive of activity: once the marching ground of the military, this square is now where Neapolitans spend their free time, with children playing, dogs running around and balloons and toys for sale. The piazza was a litter-strewn *parcheggio* (car park) until the 1990s; today it is a symbol of the city's cultural rebirth. The vehicle-free area is now a massive outdoor gallery, where internationally renowned artists such as Mimmo Paladino, Anish Kapoor, Rebecca Horn, Richard Serra or Carsten Nicolai have created impressive installations. And the New Year's Eve rave on the Piazza del Plebiscito is a mega event that one simply has to experience! ▥ f5

16 GALLERIA BORBONICA ★

The finest porcelain toilet seats can be found in this underground tunnel beneath the city's Chiaia district – the aristocracy used it as an air-raid shelter during World War II. The tunnel was originally built on orders of the king as an escape route out of the city to the sea. It was later used as a dumping ground for waste. Today, cars and motorbikes (1930–1960) are exhibited down here. Those with a head for adventure should take the *percorso avventura* rope tour, where you will be equipped with a helmet and climbing gear. *Fri–Sun 10am–5pm, varying tour start times, advance booking essential | Via Domenico Morelli 61 | galleriaborbonica.com | ⏲ 2½ hrs | ⌑ e6*

17 CASTEL DELL'OVO/ BORGO MARINARI

An interesting programme of temporary exhibitions attracts visitors to this impressive castle, which is far bigger on the inside than it appears on the outside. From the rooftop terrace you are rewarded with panoramic views of the Posillipo and of Mount Vesuvius. At the foot of the castle is Borgo Marinari, once a fishing village, today a lively meeting place with restaurants and bars. *Mon–Sat 9am–6.30pm, Sun 9am–2pm | bus 140 | ⏲ 2 hrs | ⌑ f7*

18 PAN

In the centre of the chic Chiaia quarter, the *Palazzo delle Arti di Napoli* is a forum for new, vibrant art. Creative cultural events and contemporary art shows that appeal to a wider audience are held in the 6,000m² palace. A good complement to shopping! *Mon–Fri 9.30am–7.30pm, Sat/Sun 9.30am–8.30pm | Via dei Mille 60 | comune.napoli.it/pan | Metro 1 Piazza Amedeo | ⏲ 1½ hrs | ⌑ d5*

19 MUSEO E REAL BOSCO DI CAPODIMONTE ★

Situated high above the city, the austere, red-grey former hunting lodge is home to the Bourbon kings' superb collection of paintings: Italian masters such as Titian, Mantegna, Caravaggio and many others hang in one of the world's richest art galleries. The salon made entirely of porcelain, the work of the legendary Capodimonte porcelain manufactory, is unique. Neapolitan families relax in the well-tended park full of palm trees on Sundays. The wood behind it is the green lung of the city and a joggers' paradise. *Thu–Tue 8.30am–7.30pm | Via Miano 2 | capodimonte.cultura.gov.it | Bus R 4 from Piazza Dante | ⏲ 3 hrs | ⌑ 0*

20 POSILLIPO

Along the Gulf of Naples towards the southwest is the exclusive *Posillipo* residential district: refuge of the city's wealthy residents – the nouveau rich and the old aristocratic families who left their palaces behind in the chaotic city a long time ago. The villas are set in enchanted gardens sloping down to the sea in the foothills of Monte Posillipo, and the romantic, semi-derelict *Palazzo Donn'Anna* is right on the seafront. Everything is very private, even access to the sea, although there are a few exclusive public bathing beaches, such as 🐾 *Bagno Elena (Via Posillipo 14)*. *⌑ a7*

21 MARECHIARO

Adjacent to Posillipo is the former fishing village of 🐾 *Marechiaro*, where you can sunbathe on huge boulders. Romantic seafood restaurants with a magnificent view over the gulf include *Da Cicciotto (daily | Calata Ponticello a Marechiaro 32 | tel. 08 15 75 11 65 | trattoriadacicciotto.it | €€€)*. The *Parco*

NAPLES

Let there be light: Óscar Tusquets Blanca's mosaic *Crater de Luz* in the Toledo Metro station

Sommerso di Gaiola (Daily May–Sept 9am–6pm, March/April and Oct/Nov 10am–5pm, Dec–Feb 10am–3pm | areamarinaprotettagaiola.it) was created to protect the coast and the underwater habitats. Rare ocean species make this marine reserve a paradise for divers. In the bay next to it, the *Spiaggia della Gaiola* is a favourite bathing spot for Neapolitans. *C4*

CITTÀ DELLA SCIENZA

This interesting, modern science museum is located on the western outskirts of the city. The interactive exhibits detail how our world functions: how the cosmos works, how lightning is created and what our bodies look like inside. *Mid-Sept–July Tue–Fri 9am–4pm, Sat/Sun 9am–5pm | Via Coroglio 104 | cittadellascienza.it | Metro 2 Campi Flegrei, then Bus 607 or C1 | 3 hrs | C4*

STAZIONI DELL'ARTE

The Metro Line 1 connects 11 stations exhibiting impressive works of art. The award-winning stations Toledo, Dante and Museo have been designed by artists including William Kentridge, Jannis Kounellis, Robert Wilson, Oliviero Toscani and Joseph Kosuth – which one do you like best? For the price of a metro ticket, visitors can enjoy some of the finest works of contemporary art. At the Toledo Metro station, follow the signs to the Montecalvario exit *(closed at the time of going to print, but reopening is planned)*: the portraits of everyday Neapolitans have been captured by photographer Oliviero Toscani and exhibited on the wall next to the moving walkway. *metroart.anm.it f2–4*

MURALS

The *murales* in Naples are large, created by master craftsmen and have been causing a real buzz for some time now. Crowds of art lovers from all over the world make pilgrimages to the centrally located *murales* by Francisco Bosoletti in the Spanish

Quarter: they depict a figure from the Cappella San Severo as well as the Neapolitans' football icon Diego Maradona *(Via Emanuele De Deo 46 | e4)*. The giant portrait of the city's patron saint San Gennaro by artist Jorit Agoch *(Via Duomo/Via Vicaria Vecchia | h2–3)* and his spectacular Maradona in the southeastern quarter of San Giovanni a Teduccio *(0)* are impressive, while the pictures by artist Roxy in the Box *(Vico dei Maiorani | g2)* are both witty and creative.

CATACOMBS

Next door to the Basilica della Madre del Buon Consiglio, frescoes lead down to the entrance of the underground cemetery of the early Christians, the ★ *Catacombe di San Gennaro (daily every hour on the hour 10am–5pm, online booking in advance required | Via Capodimonte 13 | catacombedinapoli.it | bus C63, 204, 168, 178 from Metro Museo, R 4 from Piazza Dante | 1½ hrs | 0)*. The four-hour tour *Il Miglio Sacro (Sun 9am)* provides a great insight into the history of all Neapolitan catacombs, the Sanità quarter and the *Cimitero delle Fontanelle* bone cemetery *(closed at the time of going to print)*. Not far away are some more catacombs, under the Santa Maria della Sanità church: *Catacombe di San Gaudosio (daily every hour on the hour 10am–1pm | Piazza Sanità 14 | 1½ hrs | f1)*. They date to the fifth century. A small bone vault *(Sun–Fri 10am–2pm, Sat 10am–5pm | Via dei Tribunali 39 | purgatorioadarco.it | g2)* can be found below the *Santa Maria delle Anime del Purgatorio ad Arco* church in the old town.

La Paranza cultural cooperative *(catacombedinapoli.it)* staff not only

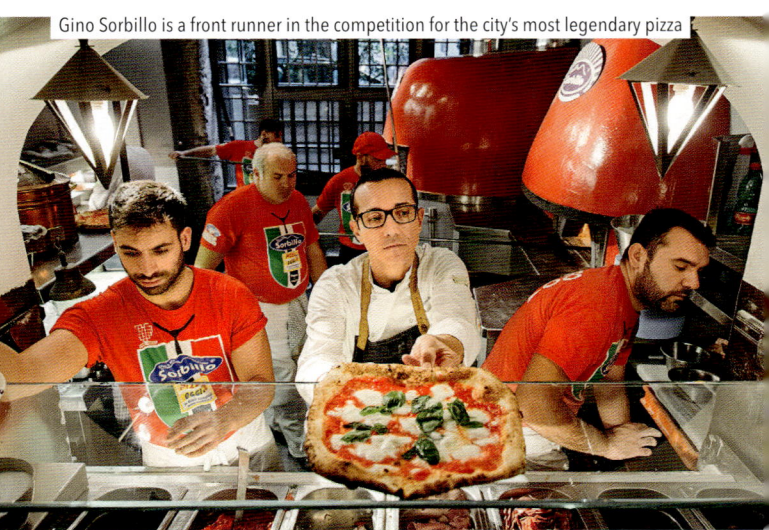

Gino Sorbillo is a front runner in the competition for the city's most legendary pizza

NAPLES

accompany visitors to the catacombs, but the organisation also offers city tours *(bookable in Italian/English via prenotazioni@catacombedinapoli.it)*, educates visitors about the social conditions in the troubled Sanità district and suggests intelligent solutions, offering the youth career prospects and alternatives to the Camorra and a life of crime.

CITY TOURS

You can explore the city on a hop-on hop-off double-decker bus tour: Line A *(65 mins)* takes you to the most important artistic sites and museums, with several museums offering a discount on presentation of the ticket. Line B *(70 mins)* runs along the coast and offers unique views of gardens and the sea. *Combined ticket 24 euros | citysightseeing.it*

INSIDER TIP: Get a bird's-eye view

EATING & DRINKING

AUGUSTUS

This is where Neapolitans go for a bite to eat at fair prices. All you can see from the outside is the bar. Just mingle with the locals and enjoy one of the delicious small dishes (takeaway also available). *Daily | Via Toledo 147 | tel. 08 15 51 35 40 | €–€€ | f4*

DA GINO SORBILLO

Legendary pizzeria dating from the 1950s, which has launched the career of a new star pizza-maker, the founder's grandson Gino. It is simply unacceptable not to try the deep-fried pizza of Gino's aunt Esterina. *Closed Sun | Via dei Tribunali 32 | tel. 0 81 44 66 43 | sorbillo.it | € | g2*

DA GIOVANNI

Trattoria in its third generation near the old fish market. Serves fresh fish in a warm atmosphere. Typical Neapolitan street flair, but only at lunchtime. *Closed Sun | Via Soprammuro a Nolana 9 | tel. 0 81 26 83 20 | € | f 0*

MAMÈ OSTRICHINA

Fancy a culinary highlight? Here you can celebrate low-carb gourmet cuisine Neapolitan-style, also vegan on request, with selected regional ingredients. Great ambience and fair prices. Booking recommended! *Closed lunchtime and Sun | Via Carlo de Cesare 52 | tel. 0 81 18 16 58 38 | FB | €€–€€€ | f5*

NENNELLA

A simple, iconic trattoria where the food is always good. It's always busy at lunchtime and in the evening. *Closed Sun | Vico Lungo Teatro Nuovo 105 | tel. 0 81 41 43 38 | € | f4*

SALVO

Pizza was originally classic street food, but there is another way: arguably the city's most elegant pizzeria (although this hardly affects the price) belongs to brothers Francesco and Salvatore, from the Salvo *pizzaioli* family, whose pizzas are a legend. *Daily | Riviera di Chiaia 271 | tel. 3 59 99 26 | pizzeria salvo.it | €–€€ | e6*

INSIDER TIP: Legendary pizza

SORRISO INTEGRALE

Vegetarian, vegan, macrobiotic and guaranteed organic: the vegetables taste particularly good at Naples' oldest organic restaurant. The owner's family is one of the largest organic vegetable growers in Italy and their fields are located near Santa Maria Capua Vetere. *Daily | Vico San Pietro a Maiella 6 | tel. 0 81 45 50 26 | sorriso integrale.com | € | ⌑ f3*

TANDEM

Young, iconic restaurant specialising in the Neapolitan ⚑ Sunday lunch classic, *ragù*, where meat is braised in tomato sauce and served with bread or pasta. A vegetarian option is also available. *Closed Wed | Via Giovanni Paladino 51 | tel. 0 81 19 00 24 68 | tandem.napoli.it | € | ⌑ g3*

RESTAQMME

Neapolitan cuisine with charm, elegantly served by Magdalena Buczynska. Local people also come here to eat. *Closed Sun evening and Mon | Via Lucilio 11 | tel. 34 25 26 85 98 | FB | €€ | ⌑ f6*

CAFÉS, PASTICCERIE, GELATERIE

You get the best espresso and the best *sfogliatelle* in Naples' oldest coffee house. The 🐗 *Gran Caffè Gambrinus (Piazza Trieste e Trento | ⌑ f5)* oozes history and 19th-century Neapolitan art adorns the walls of the big hall. During the summer you can sit at the cafés in the *Borgo Marinari (⌑ f6)* and enjoy sea views. The *Gran Caffè La Caffettiera* at the pretty *Piazza dei Martiri (⌑ e6)* in Chiaia is very chic, whereas intellectuals tend to go to the *Gourmeet Incontri di Sapore* bar *(Piazza Trieste e Trento | ⌑ f5)* at the opera house. Diagonally opposite is *Leopoldo (Via Chiaia 258 | ⌑ f5)*, one of Naples' most famous patisseries. This shop also sells spicy *taralli*, a peppery snack with almonds. Neapolitan delicacies, both sweet and savoury, are available at the trendy *Ba-Bar Officina (Via Santa Lucia 169 | ⌑ f6)*, an ideal place to relax outside.

Don Alfredo dal 1946 (⌑ f3) is a traditional juice bar in a kiosk on Piazza Dante, serving freshly squeezed orange juice and lemonade as well as delicious apple juice that's made from the Neapolitan variety of apple, *mela annurca*. Local people meet up late into the night at the ice cream parlours on the shores of Mergellina *(⌑ b7)*, especially at ⚑ *Chalet Ciro* in Via Caracciolo.

SHOPPING

A tourist highlight (and not only at Christmas) are the shops and workshops selling nativity scenes along *Via San Gregorio Armeno (⌑ g2–3)*. The exclusive fashion boutiques (all ⌑ e5-6) are found along *Via Chiaia, Via dei Mille, Via Calabritto* and *Piazza dei Martiri* in Chiaia San Ferdinando. *Studio 3 (Via Nardones 111–112 | ⌑ f5)* has cool vintage jeans and leather jackets, while *Alessandra Avallone (Via Chiaia 178 | ⌑ e5)* can make you a bespoke leather jacket at

NAPLES

an impressive price. The handmade umbrellas sold at 🌂 *Talarico (Vico Due Porte a Toledo 4b | mariotalarico.it | ⌨ f4)* in the Quartieri Spagnoli are very original. One of Naples' most creative and innovative jewellery designers is *Gustavo Renna (Via Domenico Morelli 53 | FB | ⌨ e6)*, who uses silk from the famous silk town of San Leucio to make glass gemstones and his San Gennaro rings. His washing-line necklaces are the best souvenir you can think of to take back home.

INSIDER TIP
Napoli cliché, creatively interpreted

Trendy leather bags, excellently crafted on site, can be found at *Cardone (Via Chiaia 237 | andreacardone.shop | ⌨ f5)*. There's also a *Cardone* outlet at *Via Chiaia 65 (⌨ f5)*.

Cool shirts as well as Napoli sounds ranging from folk music to hip-hop and jazz are all available from record store *Musicante (Via San Biagio dei Librai 89 | musicanteshop.it | ⌨ g3)* in the old town. Delicious handmade chocolate pralines can be bought from *Gay-Odin (branches include Via Benedetto Croce 61 | gay-odin.it | ⌨ g3)*. There are also plenty of neighbourhood markets. The *food market* on *Piazza Pignasecca (⌨ f3)* is the most versatile, while in the morning the *mercato popolare*, the *fish market* at Porta Nolana *(⌨ 0)*, is well worthwhile.

SPORT & ACTIVITIES

BICYCLES & SCOOTERS

Explore more of the city on two wheels, whether on a bicycle *(napolibike.com)*, an electric bike *(neapolisolare.it)*, a

Fancy an ice cream at 2am? No problem at Chalet Ciro in Mergellina

scooter or Vespa *(interfurnapoli.it)*. But don't forget to ask for a helmet!

KAYAK TOURS IN POSILLIPO

A kayak tour is a unique and memorable way of discovering this spectacular section of coastline, with its Roman remains. Paddle past the haunted (according to legend), ancient *Palazzo degli Spiriti* to the old fishing bay of Borgo Marechiaro. The tour lasts two to three hours and a visit to the private beach nearby as well as the cheerfulness of the young kayak people is included in the price of *30 euros. Via Posillipo 68 (entrance to Lido Le Rocce Verdi beach)* or *Bagni Elena (Via Posillipo 357) | tel. 33 88 76 11 57 | kayaknapoli.com | Bus 140 from Metro Mergellina | ⌨ 0*

INSIDER TIP
A change of perspective

STAIRWAY TOURS

More than 200 stairways cut through the city like arteries. Carmine Maturo knows them like the back of his hand and organises cleaning campaigns, stairway festivals and trekking tours up and down the flights of steps. *scaledinapoli.com, Instagram: scaledinapoli_official*

WELLNESS

PAUSILYA THERME DI DONN'ANNA A POSILLIPO

The view alone from this stylish wellness oasis right by the sea in Posillipo promises pure relaxation. Booking is essential. *Tue–Sat 10am–11pm, Sun 10am–8pm | Via Posillipo 19 | tel. 08 15 75 35 78 | pausilya.it | Bus 140 from Santa Lucia/Via Falero*

FESTIVALS

In May, Naples celebrates its cultural monuments with the *Maggio dei Monumenti,* which has guided tours, concerts, exhibitions and more. On 19 September, the feast day of San Gennaro, the whole city is in a state of heightened excitement when the miracle of the liquefaction of his blood is awaited in the cathedral.

NIGHTLIFE

The warm evenings are ideal for strolling and eating ice cream on the seafront promenade, the *lungomare (▥ c–f6)*. Young people sit on *Piazza San Domenico Maggiore (▥ g3)* in the old town while the tourists, students and arty types gather around *Piazza Bellini (▥ f2–3)*. A nightlife scene (*movida* in Italian) has developed in the Chiaia district around *Via Bisignano (▥ e6)*; the place to be seen here is the cool *L'Antiquario* club bar *(Via Vannella Gaetani 2 | ▥ e6)*: hidden behind the façade of a former antique shop, you can enjoy the best cocktails in a stylish ambience. Wine is the favourite tipple at the *Vineria L'Ebrezza di Noe (Vico Vetriera 8b | ▥ d5)* and the legendary *Vinarium (Vicolo Santa Maria Cappella Vecchia 7 | ▥ e6)*.

INSIDER TIP
Please ring the bell!

The world's oldest opera house, the *Teatro San Carlo (Via San Carlo 98F | tel. 08 17 97 24 68 | teatrosancarlo.it | ▥ f5)*, is the venue for high-quality classical music on an international level. Those who prefer cool local bands should head to *Mamamu (Via Sedile di Porto 46 | mamamu.altervista.org | ▥ g4)*. Housed in a former wool factory, the *Lanificio 25 (Piazza Enrico De Nicola 46 | lanificio25.it | ▥ h2)* draws an alternative crowd, while the historic *Jazzbar Bourbon Street (Via Vincenzo Bellini 52 | bourbonstreetjazzclub.com | ▥ f3)* keeps up with the latest jazz sounds. One popular bar on the local scene is *Made in Cloister (Piazza Enrico De Nicola 46 | madeincloister.com | ▥ h2)*, which organises concerts often at short notice. The *Gaan* nightclub *(Via Tasso 620 | FB: GAAN Clubbin'concept | ▥ 0)* is the place to be every Saturday from 9pm for over-35s who want to dance and enjoy great live music.

Some churches and *palazzi* also double up as venues for classical concerts such as the excellent concerts of

NAPLES

Spend an evening in Europe's oldest opera house, the Teatro San Carlo

ancient Neapolitan music by the *Centro Musica Antica Pietà de' Turchini* in *Santa Caterina da Siena* church *(Via Santa Caterina da Siena 38 | turchini. it | ⌖ e5)*. For programme information visit *napolike.it, napolidavivere.it* or *napolitoday.it/eventi*.

FERRIES & HYDROFOILS

Boats to Capri, Ischia and Procida as well as to Sorrento depart from *Calata Porta di Massa* (⌖ h4, car ferries), from the *Molo Beverello* (⌖ g5, hydrofoils, only to Ischia and Procida) and the *Porto Turistico Mergellina* (⌖ b7). In summer, additional hydrofoils *(metròdelmare.it)* service Naples and the towns on the coasts of Amalfi and Cilento. Information and time schedules can be found on the *Capri Schedule* app and in the daily newspapers *Il Mattino* and *La Repubblica*. Be sure to book your tickets online in advance and to collect them from the service desk at the harbour.

AROUND NAPLES

CAMPI FLEGREI (PHLEGRAEAN FIELDS)
20km to Pozzuoli, west of Naples / 40 mins by train from Garibaldi Metro station
Even if the "burning fields" no longer steam and hiss, the Solfatara of Pozzuoli, the hydrothermal lakes, ruins and damaged buildings all clearly illustrate the area's seismic activity. The

AROUND NAPLES

The Basilica Sant'Angelo in Formis contains well-preserved Byzantine frescoes

Campi Flegrei are easily accessible from Naples by metro or the Ferrovia Cumana e Circumflegrea train.

The gritty housing developments around *Pozzuoli* (pop. 81,000) have some impressive ruins from the time when the city served as a Roman port: the ruins of the massive Roman market *Macellum*, where the pillars show the effects of bradyseism – the slow lifting and lowering of the earth's surface. You can also see the massive *Anfiteatro Flavio (Wed–Mon 9am–6pm)* that dates back to CE 79. The seismic activity in the area meant that the picturesque, historic old town of Pozzuoli, located on a rocky hill, had to be vacated in 1970.

Since then, archaeological excavations at Rione Terra have uncovered a virtually intact Roman town *(daily 9am–4.30pm | Via San Filippo 1f)*.

INSIDER TIP
Time travel to antiquity

At the eastern edge of the city is the *Solfatara* (which cannot be experienced up close for the time being) – a shallow, 770m-wide and still-active crater, with hot, bubbling mud puddles and steam vents *(fumarole)* which spew sulphurous gases.

In the south, the Capo Miseno headland starts with the fishing village of *Baia*, in ancient times a fashionable resort, as evidenced by the Roman spas of the *Parco Archeologico di Baia (Tue–Sun 9am–1 hr before sunset | Via Sella di Baia 22)*. Once upon a time there were luxurious bathing villas of the Roman elite

NAPLES

all along the beach, but they have since been swallowed by the sea. You can marvel at the ruins of the ancient walls and mosaic floors that litter the seabed from the glass-bottomed 👥 excursion boat, *Cymba (departures mid-March–mid-Nov Sat noon and 3pm, Sun 10am, noon and 3pm – booking 2 days in advance essential | 15 euros, children aged 5–12 10 euros | Via Molo di Baia | tel. 34 94 97 41 83 | baiasommersa.it)*.

Back towards the north, you reach ★ *Cuma (daily 9am–2 hrs before sunset | 🗺 B4)*, the Greek Cumae (eighth century BCE), the first Greek colony on the mainland. Today it is a landscape of romantic ruins, perfectly located above the sea and shrouded in legend with the grotto of the Sibyl oracle (sixth century BCE). There are also the remains of an amphitheatre, an impressive defensive tunnel and an acropolis. 🗺 *B–C4*

CAPUA & SANTA MARIA CAPUA VETERE

40km to Capua, north of Naples / 40 mins on the A1

In the little town of Capua, you should not miss a visit to the modern *Museo Campano (Tue–Sat 9am–1.30pm, Tue and Thu also 3–5pm, Sun 9am–1pm | Via Roma 68 | museocampanocapua.it)*! It has a rich collection of artefacts and works of art from antiquity and a unique collection of votive statues in volcanic stone: mothers with babies in their arms (seventh–first century BCE) from a nearby Italian *Mater Matuta* fertility shrine, which were excavated in 1870.

Six kilometres to the northeast in Formis is the *Basilica Sant'Angelo in Formis (Mon–Fri 8am–1pm and 3–8pm, Sat/Sun 10am–12.30pm and 4–5pm)*, built in 1073. The interior is beautifully painted with well-preserved, medieval frescoes. The tour continues to the enormous 👥 Roman amphitheatre of *Santa Maria Capua Vetere (Tue–Sun 9am–1 hr before sunset)*. The most famous gladiator school, where Spartacus learnt his craft, was here in Capua. 🗺 *C–D2*

> **INSIDER TIP**
> **A monument to maternal love**

WHERE TO STAY IN NAPLES

WHAT A VIEW!

Staying overnight in Naples without a view would be a grave mistake! You are guaranteed the best views over the city to Mount Vesuvius from the boutique hotel *San Francesco al Monte (45 rooms | Corso Vittorio Emanuele II 328 | tel. 08 14 23 91 11 | sanfrancescoalmonte.it | €€–€€€ | 🗺 e4)* whose rooms were once cloister cells for the residing monks. The rooftop pool with tuff stone cave is amazing.

ON CLOUD NINE

Above the rooftops of the metropolis, yet surrounded by greenery and a garden, you can stay at simple *Casa Tolentino (13 rooms | Gradini San Nicola da Tolentino 12 | tel. 33 98 30 11 16 | mail.casatolentino.it | € | 🗺 e4)*, a former monastery.

HERCULANEUM & POMPEII

TO ANTIQUITY & BACK

Salve! After passing the ticket counter in the ruined cities of Herculaneum and Pompeii, the journey back in time begins: you walk on the same cobblestones as the people two millennia ago, look into their houses and gardens, their shops, bakeries and workshops, and visit their baths.

It seems as if the inhabitants have only recently left these places. At the same time, the two ghost towns are a reminder of the destructive forces that still lie dormant in the volcano and could be released

Probably the world's most famous place to travel back in time: Pompeii

at any time. The attraction of Pompeii and Herculaneum lies in their fantastic condition, which illustrates in amazing detail the everyday life of the ancient Romans like nowhere else. The compelling sites bring to life a world that is 2,000 years old and which, at other ruins, would only be experienced through tombs and their precious grave items or the remains of showpiece buildings.

HERCULANEUM & POMPEII

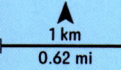

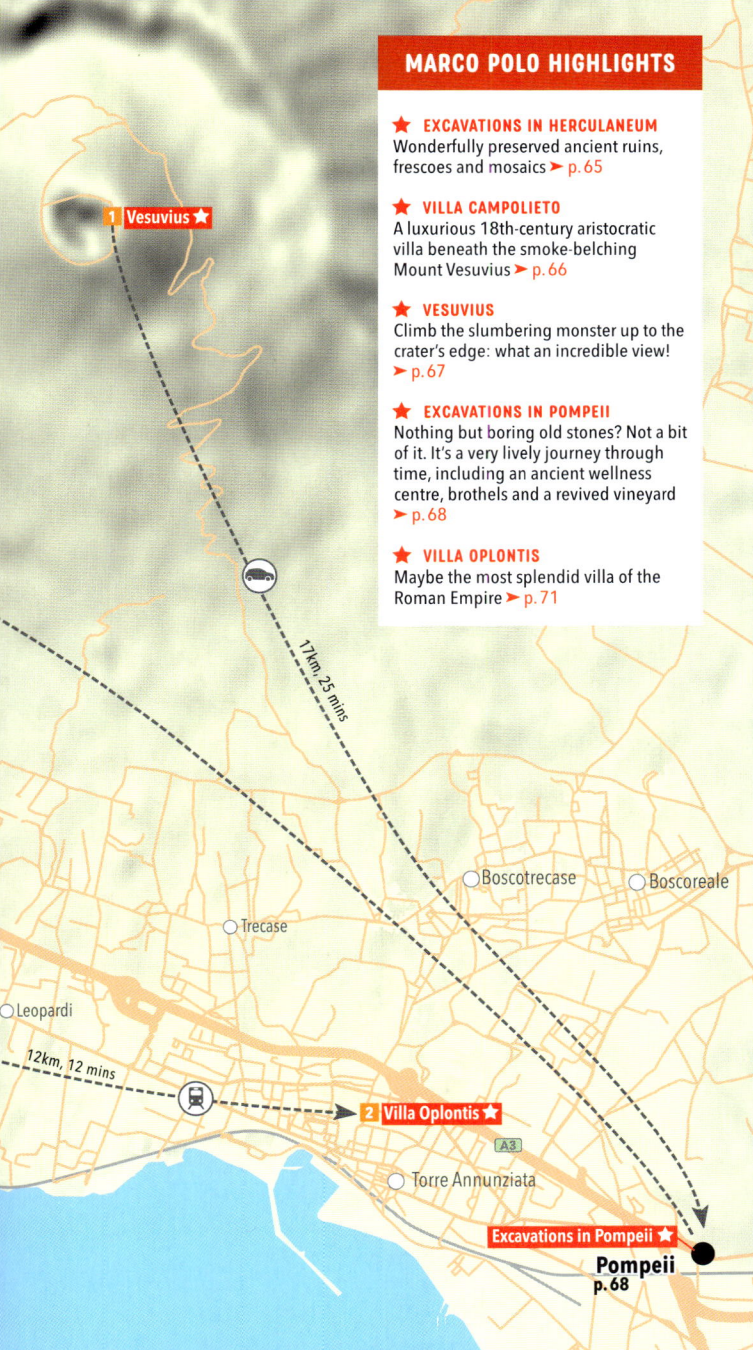

Immerse yourself in the world of the Romans! Here, you stroll through intact streets and alleys, lined with shops, workshops, bakeries and homes. The streets are paved with lava stone slabs, worn with deep grooves from the wagons of the ancient Romans and here and there you can still see the lead piping from the town's ancient aqueduct system, breaking through the high pavements.

Stucco decorations, frescoes and remnants of mosaic floors all bear witness to a strong sense of beauty and aesthetics. The luminosity of the famous deep red of the Pompeii frescoes is attributed to the fact that they added wax pigment to the limestone and soap solution and that the wall surface was smoothed with polished stones. Leisure time was also an important aspect of everyday life: in addition to a few theatres and the massive amphitheatre it is really the *palaestra* sport fields – where the young men played their sports – that attest to this. But there are also the public baths, the thermal spas and of course the *lupanari*, the brothels.

The eruption of Vesuvius began – after centuries of being dormant – on 24 August CE 79 with violent quakes. The summit of the mountain began to violently spew volcanic ash, massive dark clouds hung low, and in quick successive eruptions, glowing hot ash, boulders and *lapilli* (molten lava hardened to pumice) all rained down on the cities that lay over 10km away.

This was followed by two days of total darkness, until a pale light fought

its way through the ash cloud and by the third day the sky cleared again. Herculaneum was buried under a 20m-high layer of lava sludge and Pompeii was covered in 7m of ash and pumice. The death toll can only be an estimation, but it is believed that at least 1,500 people perished. The very volcano that had made the landscape so lush and fertile, providing such fruitful fields and vineyards, had turned the area into a desert. Ancient Stabiae, where the Sorrento Peninsula begins, was also wiped out, as well as the impressive villa complex of Oplontis, further afield.

HERCULANEUM & POMPEII

Ancient Herculaneum lies directly below the modern-day town of Ercolano

The volcanologists at the Osservatorio Vesuviano *(ov.ingv.it)* in Naples monitor Mount Vesuvius and Campi Flegrei around the clock, recording every single earth tremor. The Civil Protection Authority has prepared a contingency plan in the event that the 18 communities around Vesuvius have to be evacuated. Although it cannot be precisely predicted when earthquakes and volcanic eruptions are about to strike, it's important to recognise the signs.

Both Ercolano and Pompeii can be reached quickly (15 and 30 minutes respectively) and cheaply from Naples with the *Circumvesuviana* railway *(eavsrl.it)*. You can get a three-day combined ticket for Pompeii, Herculaneum, Villa Oplontis and Boscoreale. If you purchase tickets online (recommended), you won't have to queue *(short.travel/golf10)*. *Capri Travel Guide (capritravelguide. com)* offers interesting guided tours for children through Pompeii and Herculaneum. Please note that the numbers on the maps on p. 64 and p. 69 are for use with the map key; they do not coincide with the numbers on site.

HERCULANEUM

1. Casa di Aristide
2. Casa d'Argo
3. Casa del Genio
4. Casa dell'Albergo
5. Casa dello Scheletro
6. Casa dell'Erma di Bronzo
7. Casa a Graticcio
8. Casa del Tramezzo di Legno
9. Casa di Galba
10. Terme Urbane
11. Casa del Due Atri
12. Sacello degli Augustali
13. Casa del Salone Nero
14. Casa Sannitica
15. Casa della Stoffa
16. Casa del Mobilio Carbonizzat
17. Casa di Nettuno e Anfitrite
18. Casa del Bel Cortile
19. Casa del Bicentenario
20. Casa dell'Atrio Corinzio
21. Casa del Sacello
22. Casa del Gran Portale
23. Casa dell'Alcova
24. Casa dell'Atrio a Mosaico
25. Casa dei Cervi
26. Terme Suburbane
27. Casa della Gemma
28. Casa del Rilievo di Telefo
29. Palestra
30. Aula Superiore

HERCULAN EUM (ERCOLANO)

(□ D4) **At the time of the eruption, about 5,000 people lived in ancient Herculaneum, which was not a busy industrial centre like Pompeii, but instead was a well-kept residential area for citizens and patricians.**

The 20m-high lava sludge found its way into every house, into every crack, and turned the city into stone and cement, in the process perfectly preserving it. It is better preserved than Pompeii: here you can even see furniture, roof beams, doors (see house no.8 with a sliding door) and timber that has lasted for centuries. However, the site now has a huge problem because the excavations have exposed the materials to oxygen and the elements and decay has set in. With modern methods and good sense – hawks as pigeon control, restoration of the ancient sewerage system – the *Herculaneum Conservation Project (herculaneum.org)* has successfully managed to put a stop to the insidious destruction.

Over the centuries Herculaneum remained locked in lava and was forgotten. It became the site on which the town of *Resina*, today *Ercolano*, developed in the Middle Ages. After the first informal excavation attempts (under the Bourbon King Charles III), in 1828 layers of stone were lifted and entire houses were excavated. But it

HERCULANEUM & POMPEII

was only 100 years later that further work was conducted in a more scientific manner.

In order to excavate, the houses above the ancient city had to be demolished. The inhabitants resisted (and continue to do so) because at least two-thirds of the ancient city still serve as the foundation of the new. Unlike Pompeii, which lies on a flat area outside the new settlement, ancient Herculaneum lies beneath the present-day Ercolano, where the half-demolished houses above act like a second layer of ruins. From the long, ramp-like avenue which leads down into the ancient city, you get a good overview.

SIGHTSEEING

EXCAVATIONS ★

A street grid runs through the old city ruins, consisting of three narrow lanes, which run from south to north, called Cardo III, IV and V on the map, crossed by two broad main streets, the *Decumanus Maximus* and the *Decumanus Inferior*. Along these bumpy cobbled streets are several dozen houses. One of these expensive residential buildings is the lavish villa complex *Casa dei Cervi* (House of Deer on Cardo V, map no. 25).

On the southern side of the Cardo V are the *Terme Suburbane* (map no. 26), particularly interesting due to their

Thanks to the lava, Ercolano's mosaics are as radiant as they were two millennia ago

HERCULANEUM

thermal facilities, frescoes and floor mosaics. On Cardo IV are a few houses where some wooden furniture has miraculously been preserved; *House no. 16* has some charred furniture. In some of the villas you can even see underfloor heating, which was only available to the rich, of course.

The *Villa dei Papiri* is another highlight of the excavations. Its elegant sculptures can be viewed at the National Museum in Naples and the Greek papyrus scrolls that were found here are in the National Library in Naples. You can experience the former splendour of the villa virtually at the ★ *Museo Archeologico Virtuale (MAV) (Tue–Sun 10am–5pm | Via IV Novembre 44 | museomav.it | ⏱ 1½ hrs).* Buy your ticket online in advance to avoid the usually long queues. *April–Oct daily 8.30am–7.30pm, Nov–March Thu–Tue 8.30am–5pm | Corso Resina | ercolano.beniculturali.it | ⏱ 3 hrs*

VILLE VESUVIANE

In the 18th century, the aristocrats of the Kingdom of Naples liked to build themselves luxurious country villas in the lovely countryside with views over the gulf and the spectacularly smouldering volcano behind. Charles III had his country home, the *Palazzo Reale*, built here in *Portici* in 1738 with large parks and hunting grounds. Hundreds of villas were built between Portici and Herculaneum and the stretch was called the *Miglio d'Oro*, but one can no longer speak of the "golden mile" these days.

One hundred and twenty-two villas remain, neglected and hemmed in by modern, shabby housing developments, often built without planning permission. You can view some of them, such as the beautifully restored ★ *Villa Campolieto (Corso Resina 283)* in Herculaneum. The elegant, elliptical belvedere portico was designed by star architect Luigi Vanvitelli.

You can also visit the two nearby villas, *Villa Petti Ruggiero (Via Alessandro Rossi 42)* and *Villa Favorita (Via Gabriele D'Annunzio 36)*, which has a beautiful park. *Tue–Sun 10am–1pm | villevesuviane.net*

EATING & DRINKING

VIVA LO RE

Fine Slow Food *osteria* in an annexe of the historic Villa Campolieto, also with some stylish guest rooms. *Closed Sun evening and Mon | Corso Resina 261 | tel. 08 17 39 02 07 | vivalore.it | €€*

NIGHTLIFE

In the evening, people like to meet in the harbour of the neighbouring town of *Portici*, where the American Bar *Granhattan (Via del Porto 21)* is the place to be. A nightly doughnut, which you can get at *A'Graff (Via Libertà 59)*, is highly recommended. At weekends, the club at *Fabric Hostels (Via Bellucci Sessa 22 | fabrichostel.com)* in what used to be a weaving mill ten minutes' walk from the Portici–Via Libertà Circumvesuviana station, is often a good place to be from 10.30pm. Depending on the band, there is live rock, jazz or blues.

HERCULANEUM & POMPEII

Climb up over lava gravel to look into the mouth of the crater

AROUND HERCULANEUM

1 VESUVIUS (VESUVIO) ★
6km to the car park northeast of Ercolano / 15 mins on the Via Cupa Monti/Via Vesuvio

This dangerous 12,000-year-old volcano is not only responsible for destroying towns such as Pompeii, Herculaneum and Stabiae (in CE 79). A later eruption (in 1631) once again destroyed many of the surrounding villages and claimed an estimated 4,000 lives. The eruptions of 1906 and 1944 were also devastating. The volcano is still active today, although it seldom emits any ash. But under the 3km-deep plug of hardened lava that clogs up the 450m-deep mouth, seethes magma at a depth of 5–7km. The split into the two peaks of today, the former Monte Somma and the new crater (1,281m), happened during the eruption of CE 79. Despite the danger, the immediate surroundings around Mount Vesuvius are still densely populated, which is due to the fact that the volcano has made the soil extremely fertile. Around 700,000 people live in the 24 communities at the foot of the volcano.

You need to plan your visit to the volcano, as the ticket must be booked at *vesuviopark.vivaticket.it* the day before at the latest. The most convenient way to get to the crater is to take the road from Ercolano that ends in a car park. A chargeable shuttle bus takes you to the entrance. Alternatively, there is a bus *(vesuvioexpress.info)* from the Ercolano Scavi stop on the Circumvesuviana railway. From the pay desk, it is another 40-minute walk across lava fields to the rim of the crater.

Vesuvius is now a national park with 11 signposted hiking trails (totalling a good 50km). You can buy a route map at the info point at the car park where the shuttle bus starts, and the website *short.travel/golf21* provides an overview. On the road from Herculaneum to Vesuvius is the 1841 seismological observation station, the *Osservatorio Vesuviano (currently closed for restoration work | ov.ingv.it)*. It is the oldest scientific institution for the study of a volcano (there's a historical exhibition on site).

Once on the edge, you will be able see down into the crater where there are a few isolated vents with plumes of steam. The view from the crater is overwhelming, but the climb is only advisable when the weather is calm and visibility is good. Sturdy footwear is required. *Guided tours daily 9am to 2 hrs before sunset | vesuviopark.it |* ⏱ *3 hrs | E4*

POMPEII

(E5) **While more than 3.5 million people from all over the world come to Pompeii every year to visit the ancient city (book online to avoid long queues!), over four million visitors, mainly Italians, come to visit the vast pilgrimage church of the Madonna of the Rosary.**

At the time Pompeii was buried under ash and pumice in CE 79, it was already an old, established town. The people of Pompeii produced and traded wine, oil, olives, wheat, fabric, wool, bricks and much more. Today's Pompeii (pop. 25,000) was created at the time of the first excavations in the late 18th century; its centre is the 🚩 pilgrimage church *Santuario della Madonna del Rosario (santuario.it)* on the large piazza. Impressive communal prayers are held on 8 May and on the first Sunday in October, and car blessings (no joke!) take place every weekday from 9am to 12.30pm and 4.30pm to 6.30pm, with longer hours at weekends. We recommend booking online: *short.travel/golf20*

INSIDER TIP — A show of faith

SIGHTSEEING

EXCAVATIONS ⭐

It's best to enter the ruined city through the *Porta Marina*, but before then a visit to the *Terme Suburbane* – outside the city walls – is a must. The luxurious public bathing facilities even had its own jetty, the interior

HERCULANEUM & POMPEII

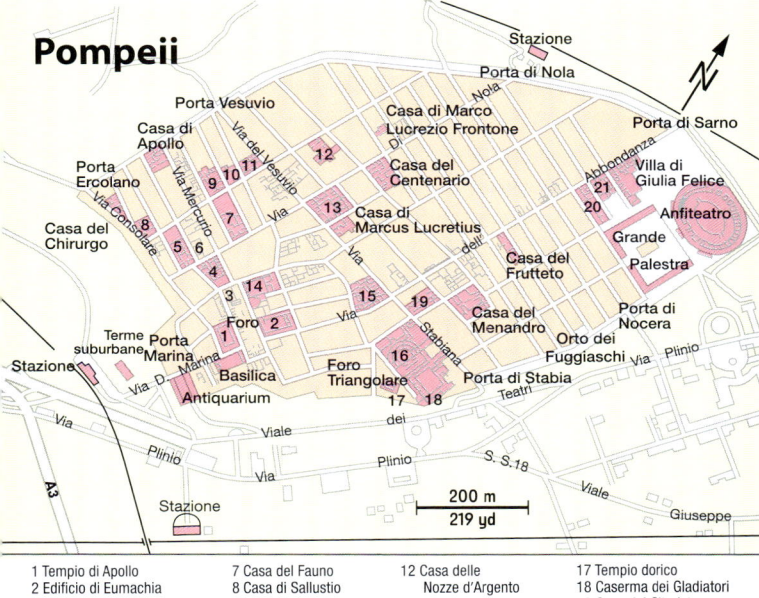

1 Tempio di Apollo
2 Edificio di Eumachia
3 Tempio di Giove
4 Terme del Foro
5 Casa di Pansa
6 Casa del Poeta tragico
7 Casa del Fauno
8 Casa di Sallustio
9 Casa del Labirinto
10 Casa dei Vettii
11 Casa degli Amorini dorati
12 Casa delle Nozze d'Argento
13 Terme centrali
14 Macellum
15 Terme Stabiane
16 Teatro Grande
17 Tempio dorico
18 Caserma dei Gladiatori
19 Casa del Citarista
20 Casa di Marcus Loretus Tiburtinus
21 Casa di Venere

walls are covered in refined stucco decorations, and the changing-room walls have erotic illustrations which are believed to help bathers remember which boxes or lockers were theirs. Here, travellers who found the city gates closed at a late hour could find a place of rest. Behind the city gate, after a few shops, you reach the area with the public buildings and squares: to the right, the large, three-aisled *Basilica*, back then the seat of the court and a meeting room; to the left, the extensive *Forum* with the Temple of Jupiter and Apollo. One of the market halls is also on the right. This is where the Pompeiians met every day.

Further on is *Via dell'Abbondanza* and the main shopping street in antiquity, *Decumanus Maximus*, with its homes and shops, and the large public baths *Terme Stabiane* that face a small alley that leads to the left, to the *lupanare* (brothels). On the right of the main street is the theatre district with a small and large *theatre*, the *gladiator barracks* and the *Temple of Isis*, whose marvellous, almost intact frescoes can now be seen in the National Museum of Naples. The Via dell'Abbondanza leads to the other end of the town, the *Porta di Sarno*, past the wool-cleaning and dyeing area, *Stephani*, to the large sports

POMPEII

fields, the *palaestra*, and the huge 20,000-seater *amphitheatre*.

In front of the sporting ground you turn right to the town's ancient vineyards, some of which have been replanted with ancient Aglianico and Piedirosso vines. During the time of the Roman Empire, Pompeii was Rome's main source of wine. Today, visitors are sometimes able to witness the grape harvest that takes place every autumn and is a special experience. The vineyards in and around Pompeii will soon cover almost seven hectares, and winegrowers and archaeologists will once again cultivate vines. It is a scientific project that aims to produce wine in the archaeological park using ancient, organic cultivation methods. In one of the gardens, the *orto dei fuggiaschi*, you will encounter a glass case which contains the very moving casts of the men, women and children who died while trying to escape the ash rain.

INSIDER TIP
Wine as it was 2,000 years ago

The southwestern part of the town has the largest number of magnificent private villas, most notably the *Casa dei Dioscuri* and the *Casa dei Vettii*. The largest villa in the city is the *Casa del Fauno*. (The original statue of the dancing faun can be found in the museum in Naples, as can the Alexander Floor Mosaic.) The restored *House of Marco Lucrezio Frontone* is well worth seeing, especially the ochre-yellow room containing frescoes of miniature landscapes and poignant portraits of children, assumed to be those of the house's former residents.

INSIDER TIP
Immerse yourself in daily Roman life

A stroll along the walls around Pompeii, the *Passeggiata fuori le Mura* will give you a fantastic view of the ruined city. An absolute must-see is the *Villa dei Misteri* just outside the city walls, in the southwest. The

Villa dei Misteri: frescoes believed to be showing initiation rites

HERCULANEUM & POMPEII

beautiful second-century villa in the countryside has still not revealed all its secrets: what are the people in the frescoes doing – especially the women? Why does everyone depicted in the villa's wonderful frescoes appear so tense – or is it so melancholic? There are numerous interpretations, but the common belief among experts is that the frescoes depict preparations for a Dionysian initiation rite.

To preserve the mosaics on the floor and the frescoes, not all rooms are accessible. The helpful audio guides and free maps with explanations are available at the entrance of Piazza Porta Marina. Downloadable maps of all the archaeological sites, various suggested routes (two, three or five hours) and a list of all the open houses can be found on the website. To ensure that a visit to Pompeii with a pushchair (all-terrain only!) does not turn into an ordeal, we recommend the shorter tour from the Piazza Anfiteatro entrance. *Daily 9am–5pm, April–Oct until 7pm, some of the houses may only be open in the morning due to a lack of staff | pompeiisites.org | ◔ at least 2 hrs*

EATING & DRINKING

GARUM
Excellent restaurant named after the fermented fish sauce popular in the times of ancient Pompeii. It is advisable to book a table! *Closed Sun evening and Wed | Via Mazzini 63 | tel. 08 18 50 11 78 | ristorantegarumpompei.it | €-€€*

IL PRINCIPE
Cuisine inspired by Roman antiquity in the centre of modern Pompeii, but not far from the Porta di Nocera entrance to the excavations. Head chef and landlord Gianmarco Carli serves delicious snacks in the wine bar. *Closed Sun evening and Wed | Via Colle San Bartolomeo 4 | tel. 08 18 50 55 66 | ilprincipe.com | €€€*

AROUND POMPEII

2 VILLA OPLONTIS ★
5km northwest of Pompeii / 15 mins on the SS 18

In the middle of *Torre Annunziata*, one of those rather shabby towns along the gulf coast, lies what is probably the most beautiful villa of the Roman period – buried by Vesuvius's CE 79 eruption. One must imagine that this beautiful country estate, with its brightly painted rooms, courtyards, baths, pools (the main pool measured 61m by 17m!) and gardens was once in the middle of a lush, green landscape overlooking the sea. So far nearly two-thirds of the estate has been excavated. This grandiose and well-preserved villa – said to have belonged to Poppea, the wife of Nero – is not on the main tourist trail, making a visit a very special experience. *Wed–Mon 9am–5pm, April–Oct until 7pm | Via dei Sepolcri | pompeiisites.org | ◔ 1½ hrs | ⌘ E5*

INSIDER TIP
As a guest of the empress

CAPRI, ISCHIA, PROCIDA

A BEAUTIFUL, CONTRASTING TRIO OF ISLETS

No matter which island you visit, welcome to paradise! There's a sophisticated lifestyle on the Piazzetta of Capri, healing springs on Ischia and idyllic living under lemon trees on Procida.

Each of the three islands in the Gulf of Naples is a small world of its own, appealing to a different type of traveller. Attracted by the Grotta Azzurra (Blue Grotto), thousands of day trippers flood Capri in summer. Those who love thermal baths and are looking for a varied

At Punta Tragara, you have the perfect view of Capri's landmark, the Faraglioni

holiday destination come to Ischia. Procida, on the other hand, is an oasis for nature lovers.

Incidentally, Capri town is completely car-free, as is the centre of Anacapri and the town centres of Lacco Ameno and Sant'Angelo on Ischia. The best way to get around is on foot or by bus and taxi. Exploring the islands by bike is a great experience; you can hire bicycles, scooters or e-bikes in all harbours. For information on ferry connections see p. 132.

CAPRI, ISCHIA, PROCIDA

MARCO POLO HIGHLIGHTS

★ **CAPRI**
The world-famous island is a small paradise for hikers and bon vivants
➤ p. 76

★ **SAN MICHELE**
Beautiful majolica-tile floor in a Capri church ➤ p. 77

★ **LA MORTELLA**
Exotic, Mediterranean garden paradise on Ischia ➤ p. 80

★ **NEGOMBO**
Thermal spa with a meditative, Zen-like atmosphere in a beautiful bay on Ischia
➤ p. 81

★ **CORRICELLA**
The fishing village on Procida is both an oasis and a film set ➤ p. 83

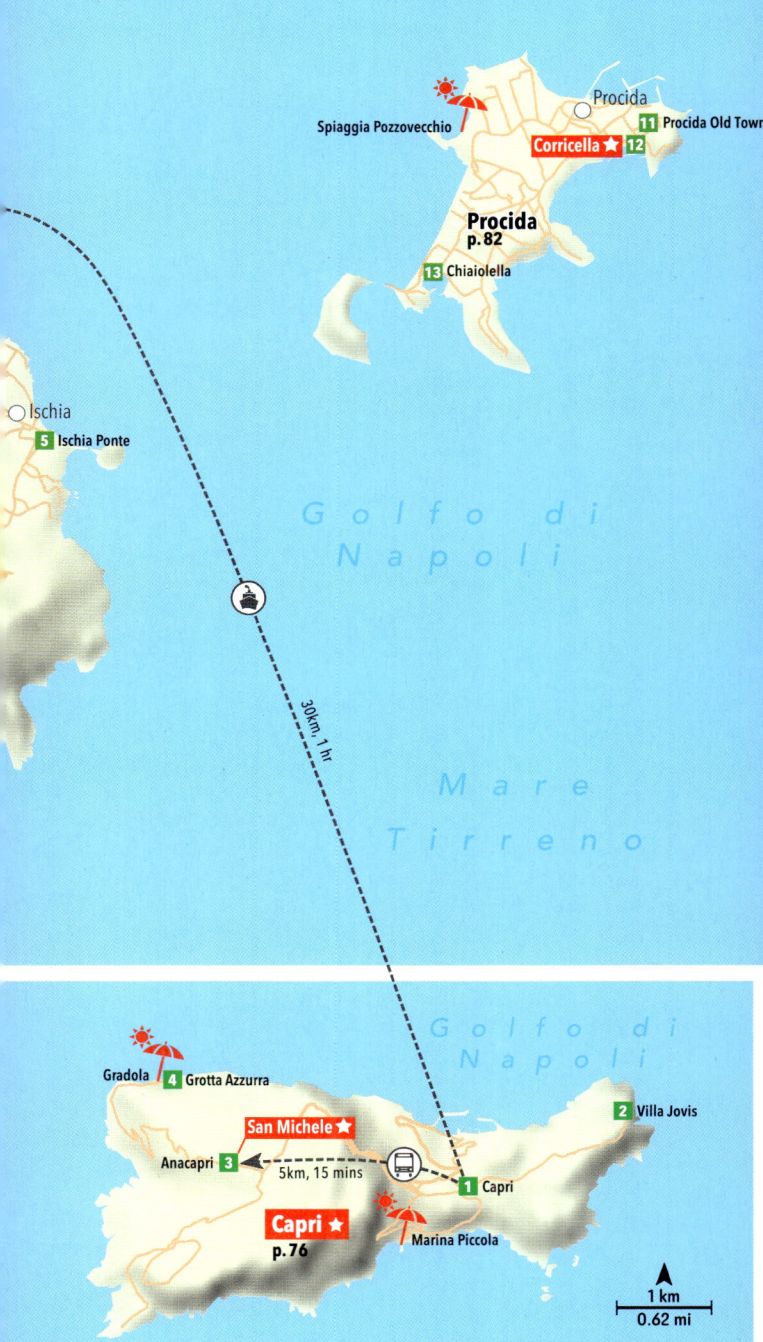

CAPRI

All visitors arrive here: Capri's Marina Grande

CAPRI

(*C-D 6-7*) **Benvenuto! Welcome to the most exclusive ★ island in the Gulf of Naples. Just 10km² in size, this block of light-coloured limestone off the tip of the Sorrento Peninsula boasts two villages situated on high plateaux.**

The first is the capital *Capri* with its winding alleyways, fine boutiques, elegant hotels and the Marina Grande harbour, where the ferries dock, and Marina Piccola, the picturesque bay on the southern side. The second is *Anacapri*, larger and more spread out, greener, more rural, and not as sophisticated. The island was discovered by the Roman Emperor Augustus. Emperor Tiberius spent 14 years on the island, enchanted by the beautiful views as well as the bizarre rock formations of the Faraglioni and the Arco Naturale, but also by the many grottos, among them the Grotta Azzurra, the Blue Grotto, which he used for rituals and celebrations.

ISLAND WALK

The quickest way to escape Capri's day trippers is on foot, and at the same time you will get to know the most beautiful corners of the island. Simply follow the blue ceramic signs, such as the one from La Croce to the west on the Via Matermania in the direction of the Arco Naturale. At the restaurant Le Grottelle, the path can be continued as a loop past the Grotta di Matermania and above the spectacularly situated

CAPRI, ISCHIA, PROCIDA

Casa Malaparte to the Belvedere di Tragara lookout point, where – after one and a half hours – you're back in town.

DESTINATIONS ON CAPRI

1 CAPRI

From *Marina Grande* – with its ferry piers, excursion boats and yachts, a few cafés, restaurants and a narrow strip of pebbly beach – you can walk via a stepped path into the heart of Capri (pop. 7,200) or you can take the quicker route up by cable car (at the top station is a left-luggage storage place for day visitors).

The centre of town is the famous *Piazzetta (Piazza Umberto I)*. During the day, the place is crowded with day trippers but in the evenings it becomes a charming meeting place for permanent guests, the jet-set and the locals. The picturesque town is the perfect mixture of a Mediterranean maze of alleyways and elegant hotels, restaurants, boutiques and jewellers. You can buy original and sophisticated souvenirs at *Eco Capri (Piazzetta Ignazio Cerio 11)*, with accessories, fashion and objects by the Capri-based artist Laetitia Cerio.

INSIDER TIP: Island history to take away

One attraction is the *Carthusian Monastery of San Giacomo (Tue–Sun 10am–6pm | Via Certosa 10)*, an impressive 14th-century monastery complex which is now used for cultural events. The monastery is built on the remains of one of the 12 villas of Emperor Tiberius. There is a *permanent exhibition* in the refectory with enormous paintings by German artist Karl Wilhelm Diefenbach, who lived on the island from 1899 until his death in 1913.

The steep serpentine cliff path, the *Via Krupp*, begins at the panoramic gardens *Giardini di Augusto*. The German industrialist, Alfred Krupp, had the switchback footpath carved into the cliff in 1902. It snakes down for about a mile to the popular *Marina Piccola* swimming bay, although it is sometimes closed due to danger of falling rocks. In the bay the three *Faraglioni* sea stacks – Capri's famous landmarks – rise from the ocean.

2 VILLA JOVIS

Of the 12 villas on Capri built by Emperor Tiberius in CE 27–37 (when he ruled the Roman Empire from here), *Villa Jovis* is the most magnificent. The remains of the villa, which is thought to have had eight floors, include most of its walls, cisterns and thermal baths. A 45-minute walk leads through the lush villa gardens to the beautifully exposed ruins. *March–Oct Thu–Sun 10am–6pm, in summer until 6.30pm*

3 ANACAPRI

In the village of Anacapri (pop. 7,000) make a stop at the ★ *San Michele* church *(April–Sept daily 9am–7pm, Oct–March 10am–3pm | chiesa-san-michele.com)* with its wonderful majolica floor, where the expulsion of Adam and Eve from the Garden of Eden is depicted in colourful detail. There is also the perfectly positioned *Villa San Michele (daily May–Sept 9am–6pm, April and Oct 9am–5pm, March 9am–4.30pm, Nov–Feb 9am–3.30pm | Via*

CAPRI

Capodimonte | villasanmichele.eu) built in 1896 as the summer home of Swedish doctor and writer Axel Munthe. A shopping lane leads to the villa. In its park you can see why everyone raves about this place: the view is unique.

Various, poorly signposted trails lead up *Monte Solaro* (589m), but the mountain is also accessible by chairlift. Here you'll find the medieval hermitage of *Santa Maria a Cetrella*, with a Madonna shrine in an idyllic setting with breathtaking views of the island, as well as the viewing terrace *Belvedere della Migliara* overlooking the steep rocky coast. For some tasty country cuisine, five pretty rooms and a swimming pool with views as far as Ischia (also for day guests), try *Da Gelsomina alla Migliara (April–Dec daily | tel. 08 18 37 14 99 | dagelsomina.com | €€€)*.

INSIDER TIP
Bird's-eye views of Capri

INSIDER TIP
Panoramic pool

4 GROTTA AZZURRA 🚩
Arguably the most famous grotto in the world. The seawater has an intense turquoise colour! You can reach the it from Marina Grande *(boat trip incl. entrance fee 34 euros)* or from Anacapri. The walk from Anacapri takes about 45 minutes, but you can also take the public bus from the village centre and there are excursion boats at the pier *(incl. entrance fee approx. 14 euros)*. A little further on is *Gradola*, a popular but tiny rocky plateau for the best jump into the sea. *Daily 9am–sunset, rough seas*

INSIDER TIP
Azure sea!

mean that it is not always accessible; info: tel. 08 18 37 06 86.

EATING & DRINKING

BUONOCORE 🚩
The speciality of this historic ice-cream parlour is their "Fantasia di Capri". *Closed Tue | Via Vittorio Emanuele 35*

DA GEMMA
The *Le Ondine* beach resort is located on the pebble beach of Marina Grande. It includes this cool lounge bar with a restaurant and views of the Neapolitan coast. *Easter–early Oct daily | tel. 08 12 77 90 56 | dagemma.com | €€*

LO SFIZIO
Unpretentious family trattoria on the way to Villa Jovis, recommended by the locals. Pizza in the evenings. *Closed Nov–Easter, except July/Aug closed Tue | Via Tiberio 7e | tel. 08 18 374128 | losfiziocapri.com | €–€€*

PULALLI WINE BAR
Perched above the Piazzetta like a bird's nest is this wine bar at the top of the clock tower, serving the finest Caprese cuisine accompanied by selected wines. It's a popular place, so remember to book a table on the terrace in advance. *Closed Tue and Nov–Easter | Piazzetta Umberto I | tel. 08 18 3741 08 | €€–€€€*

INSIDER TIP
High above the Piazzetta

TERRAZZA BRUNELLA
As charming as it is elegant: a restaurant with refined Caprese cuisine and selected wines, but the highlight is

CAPRI, ISCHIA, PROCIDA

the unforgettable view of Marina Piccola bay! *Mid-April–Oct daily | Via Tragara 24 | tel. 08 18 37 01 22 | villabrunella.it | €€€*

SPORT & ACTIVITIES

CHARLIE RENT A SCOOTER

Do you want to get a quick overview of the island? Then hire a scooter or an e-bike, which can also be delivered to you at the harbour on request. *Capri | Via Roma 70 | tel. 08 18 37 58 63 | caprirentscooter.com*

BEACHES

Near the *Marina Grande* is the *Bagni di Tiberio (bagnitiberio.com)*, a beach resort and restaurant that has retained its 1960s charm. A shuttle boat from Marina Grande will take you there in five minutes. On the south side opposite is the Marina Piccola and below the Punta di Tragara are some exclusive bathing resorts on the rocky slabs, including the renowned *La Fontelina*. At the other end of the island, the southwest tip, you can swim in the sea and eat well, including at the *Lido del Faro* beach resort *(lido-faro.com)* in a rocky bay near the lighthouse at Punta Carena *(taxi or bus from Cimitero station in Anacapri)*.

ISCHIA

(A–B5) **Ischia (pop. 67,000, 46.3km²) is the largest of the islands in the Gulf of Naples and, together with Procida, lies at the northern arc of the gulf.**

A visit to Villa San Michele is worthwhile for the fabulous views of the island alone

ISCHIA

The island owes its fame to its volcanic nature: it has an extinct volcano, Mount Epomeo, craters (including underwater craters), 103 hot springs, 69 fumarole fields and volcanic mud – making it a major attraction for tourists. The island was also popular with the Romans, who came here for thermal treatments. Today, it has over 400 hotels catering to 3.4 million tourists who still come annually for spa treatments. Aside from its beaches and thermal treatments, Ischia offers many hiking trails, such as the hike from Fontana up *Epomeo* (788m).

DESTINATIONS ON ISCHIA

5 ISCHIA PONTE & ISCHIA PORTO

The island's capital, Ischia, lies in the northeast and has two distinct centres: picturesque *Ischia Ponte* and the harbour quarter *Ischia Porto*, with a lively entertainment mile, known as the Rive Droite. Here you'll find the popular *Trattoria Antonio (April–Oct daily | Via Porto 55 | tel. 0 81 98 42 64 | €€)*. Ischia Ponte is the small rock island joined to Ischia by a bridge, with the 🎭 *Castello Aragonese (daily 9am–sunset | castelloaragoneseischia.com | ⏱ 2 hrs)*, which is especially worth discovering with children (evening ghost hunts in summer by appointment).

6 CASAMICCIOLA

Casamicciola is a relatively modern town. Most of the thermal springs are here, so it tends to be the main destination for tourists on spa package tours. The historic *Manzi Therme (hoteltermemanzi.it)* reopened as a luxury hotel, and you can visit the spa by appointment.

7 LACCO AMENO

Lacco Ameno is also exclusive, with villas, luxurious hotels and boutiques. The international jet-set has been coming here since the 1950s, after the famous publisher Angelo Rizzoli discovered the fishing village. His *Villa Arbusto (daily 9am–1.45pm, Tue–Sun 3–6.45pm | beniculturali.it)* is now a museum with archaeological treasures. The promenade by the marina is ideal for an evening stroll.

8 FORIO

Forio was an artist's enclave during the 1950s, and in the lively old town centre you can find the picturesque little *Santa Maria del Soccorso* church and two beautiful, sandy beaches: *Spiaggia di Citara* and *Spiaggia di San Francesco*. North of Forio is the enchanting ⭐ 🚩 *La Mortella (April–Oct Tue, Thu, Sat, Sun 9am–7pm | Via Francesco Calise 45 | lamortella.org)*, a subtropical and Mediterranean garden with a teahouse and concert programme.

9 SANT'ANGELO

The former fishing village of Sant'Angelo is another popular destination. Its simple white and pastel-coloured houses hug the hillside and are criss-crossed by narrow alleyways and steps that lead down to the sea. In the foreground is the small, wooded peninsula of *Punta*

CAPRI, ISCHIA, PROCIDA

Sant'Angelo with its castle ruin. Sant'Angelo also has the lovely, sandy beach 🚩 *Spiaggia dei Maronti*, where underground volcanic activity heats up the dark sand. Further west, at *Sorgeto Bay* (3km south of Panza or by boat from Sant'Angelo) you will find natural thermal baths where hot springs mix with the sea water.

WELLNESS

THERMAL SPAS

The thermal spa in Sant'Angelo is *Aphrodite Apollon (miramaresearesort.it)*; the *Parco Castiglione (SS 270 at Punta la Scrofa | termecastiglione.it)* in Casamicciola is quite expensive; while the *Giardini di Poseidon (giardiniposeidonterme.com)* at Forio's Citara beach is a garden oasis. In the centre of Ischia Porto is the modern *Terme di Ischia (Via delle Terme 15 | termeischia.eu)* open throughout the year. Tucked into the picturesque bay of San Montano is the wonderful thermal park ★ *Negombo (negombo.it)* at Lacco Ameno with an excellent terrace restaurant (€€). 🚩 The fango bath at the *Terme Cava Scura (cavascura.it/terme)* in the tuff rocks above Maronti Beach is a

These days bathing is the main activity in the former fishing village of Sant'Angelo

🔟 BARANO

The municipality of Barano is the centre of Ischia's culinary traditions, with its vineyards and the popular local speciality, a particularly delicious wild rabbit stew – the best version is served at *Il Focolare (closed Wed and lunchtime except Sat/Sun | Via Cretajo al Crocefisso 3 | tel. 0 81 90 29 44 | €-€€)*, which is run by the D'Ambra family – Slow Food at its tastiest!

INSIDER TIP
Wonderful fango mud

PROCIDA

![Hot baths provide relaxation: Giardini di Poseidon thermal spa park]

<mark>memorable experience.</mark> The thermal parks are generally open from April to October, day entrance fee: from 32 euros.

PROCIDA

(□ B5) **It will only take you 30 minutes by hydrofoil to escape the busy chaos of Naples and reach the calm of affordable Procida.**

The island may be small (4km²) but it has everything: magical bays, dreamy hillsides with breathtaking sea views, delicious food and 10,000 hospitable islanders make it the perfect island getaway. Like Ischia, Procida is a volcanic island which means it is extremely fertile, as you can see from the delightful lemon groves. However, in the month of August, the island belongs to the Neapolitans, who come here for their summer break. Ferries run several times a day from Pozzuoli, Naples and Ischia.

DESTINATIONS ON PROCIDA

11 OLD TOWN

The old town, *Terra Murata*, lies on the highest point (90m) of the island. From the harbour – with its fishermen's houses and a few restaurants and cafés – it only <mark>takes a few minutes by e-bike to get up to the *Palazzo D'Avalos* fortress on a steep cliff.</mark>  **INSIDER TIP: Great views by e-bike** <mark>From here you can enjoy a magnificent view of the Gulf of Naples and the island,</mark> with its light-coloured houses set in lush citrus gardens. *Sprint (Via*

CAPRI, ISCHIA, PROCIDA

Roma 28 | tel. 33 98 65 96 00 | from 25 euros/day) will bring you a bike directly to the harbour.

12 CORRICELLA ⭐

At the foot of the mountain lies the fishing village of *Corricella*, its colourful little houses and blue boats making it the most picturesque corner of Procida. Here, fishermen still mend their nets and laundry dangles in front of the houses – no wonder that film directors such as Anthony Minghella and Michael Radford have discovered it as the perfect backdrop. In *The Talented Mr Ripley* and *Il Postino* (The Postman), Corricella awakens a longing for southern Italy.

13 CHIAIOLELLA

Another harbour village, *Chiaiolella*, lies at the other end of the island in a small bay, with beaches, hotels and the offshore island of *Vivara*, a nature reserve and bird sanctuary.

EATING & DRINKING

DA MARIA

INSIDER TIP
Fresh from the sea

Host Maria welcomes guests at her restaurant on the harbour front in the bay of Corricella. She is Procida's one and only fisherwoman and a talented cook. When it rains, the kitchen remains closed – but that rarely happens. *Oct-April closed Mon-Fri | Marina Corricella 36 | tel. 33 88 13 0139 | €-€€*

LA PERGOLA

Delicious Mediterranean cuisine served under lemon trees in the centre of the island. *Closed Mon in winter | Via Salette 10 | tel. 08 18 96 99 18 | €*

BEACH

SPIAGGIA POZZOVECCHIO 🌴

In the northwest of the island, sheltered in a wide bay, lies what is probably Procida's most beautiful beach with dark sand and surrounded by Mediterranean vegetation.

WHERE TO STAY ON ISCHIA & PROCIDA

SO CLOSE TO THE SEA

On Ischia, you can fulfil your dream of staying in a hotel that is located directly on the beach, with both a pool and a beach bathing area, as well as state-of-the-art spa treatments. The location on Spiaggia Maronti near Barano is hard to beat. *Hotel Parco Smeraldo Terme (65 rooms | Via Maronti 42 | tel. 0 81 99 01 27 | hotelparcosmeraldo.com | €€-€€€)*

MAKE YOURSELF AT HOME ON PROCIDA

Enjoy a home from home on Procida in the 20 centrally located *Gioia Apartments (Via Flavio Gioia 37 | tel. 0 81 18 92 18 66 | gioiapartments.it | €)*, which are simple, reasonably priced and ideal for families.

SORRENTO & THE AMALFI COAST

MAGICAL MOUNTAINS & DIVINE COAST

In ancient times, mule tracks in the mountains connected the coastal villages. So beautiful was the scenery that the locals believed the gods must live up there, which is why the coast is called *La Divina Costiera*, the Divine Coast.

It begins with the foothills of the Monti Lattari, the mountains that push into the sea as a peninsula and form the southern arch of the Gulf of Naples, and ends at the ceramics town of Vietri sul Mare. The Amalfi Coast used to attract painters and intellectuals, but since the

The Amalfi Coast near Positano is appropriately marketed as *La Divina Costiera*

1950s, stars and starlets from all over the world have flocked to the Amalfi Coast. Luckily, UNESCO protects the rugged rocky landscape as a World Heritage Site.

The glittering, cobalt-blue sea is also to be preserved: a marine reserve stretches from Massa Lubrense to Positano. Because the whole world wants to come to this divine region, the Amalfitana (Amalfi Drive), the 42km-long coastal road, is no longer the dream it used to be; but there are boats as an alternative!

SORRENTO & THE AMALFI COAST

- Portici
- Terzigno
- Poggiomarino
- Sant'Antonio
- Camaldoli della Torre
- Trecase
- Pellegrini
- Marchesa
- Boscotrecase
- Boscoreale
- Santa Maria La Bruna
- Leopardi
- San Pietro
- Pompei
- Torre Annunziata
- Scafati
- Rovigliano
- Santa Maria la Carità

Golfo di Napoli

- Pioppaino
- Casola di Napoli
- Castellammare di Stabia
- Gragnano
- Pimonte
- Vico Equense
- Sant' Andrea
- **Monte Faito** [1]
- Seiano
- Moiano
- Montechiaro
- Fornacelle
- Ticciano
- Preazzano
- Meta
- Arola
- Sant'Agnello
- Piano di Sorrento
- **Sorrento** p. 88
- 16km, 40 mins
- **Positano** p. 92
- [4] Montepertuso
- [4] Spiaggia d'Arienzo
- Bomera
- Massa Lubrense
- **Locanda Don Alfonso 1890** ★
- Western Amalfitana [5]
- **Sant'Agata sui Due Golfi** [2]
- Praiano
- 20km, 55 mins
- Torca
- Termini
- Nerano [3]
- [3] Marina del Cantone
- [3] Punta Campanella

Mare Tirreno

4 km / 2.49 mi

MARCO POLO HIGHLIGHTS

★ **LOCANDA DON ALFONSO 1890**
World-class Mediterranean cuisine in an idyllic village ➤ p. 91

★ **DUOMO SANT'ANDREA**
A touch of the Orient in Amalfi's cathedral ➤ p. 96

★ **ANTICHI SENTIERI**
Hike along the old mule tracks surrounded by wonderful nature and breathtaking views ➤ p. 98

★ **TERRAZZA DELL'INFINITO**
As the name suggests, Ravello's viewing terrace has never-ending views over the coast and the sea ➤ p. 103

★ **DUOMO DI SALERNO**
Salerno's Romanesque cathedral has Arabic-style pillars and beautiful Baroque decor ➤ p. 104

SORRENTO

(□ E6) **Thanks to their fantastic location on a vast volcanic plateau high above the Gulf of Naples, Sorrento (pop. 17,000) and its peninsula were "discovered" by the English in the 18th century and soon became a popular destination.**

In the years that followed, lush parks were created and grand hotels and beautiful villas were built. Some of these are still standing and they give Sorrento an old-world magic. Many new hotels (and even campsites) have been added over time and the plateau has the usual urban sprawl and traffic chaos. Sorrento is also a centre for the art of intricately detailed wood inlay or intarsia. And, given its proximity to Naples and the Amalfi Coast, there is even a nightlife scene with clubs and wine bars.

SIGHTSEEING

MUSEO BOTTEGA DELLA TARSIA LIGNEA
The Renaissance palace Pomarici Santomasi is in itself worth a visit, but it also exhibits a remarkable collection of inlay work collected by the inlay artist Alessandro Fiorentino, along with some of his own design pieces. Here you will learn to detect counterfeit from genuine inlay works. There is also a shop. *Daily 10am–6pm | Via San Nicola 28 | museomuta.it | ⓧ 30 mins*

SEDILE DOMINOVA
In the 16th century, aristocratic city councillors held their meetings under this loggia, painted with frescoes; today pensioners from the workers' union sit and play cards. *Via San Cesareo 72*

CHURCHES
The Romanesque *Santi Filippo e Giacomo* cathedral on the *Corsa Italia* has a façade that was added in 1924 and old and new inlay work in the interior and on the portal. The Arabic-style *San Francesco* cloister is the site of summer concerts. The *Sant'Antonio* church houses votive images of seafarers and a beautiful nativity scene.

SORRENTO & THE AMALFI COAST

From Sorrento, the view sweeps across the Gulf of Naples to Mount Vesuvius

BELVEDERE AT VILLA COMUNALE
This splendid lookout terrace has panoramic views 🐾; it is in Sorrento's small city park, a former monastery garden.

MUSEO CORREALE DI TERRANOVA
In a villa with a wonderful lemon grove (which is worth a visit in itself because of the beautiful views from the belvedere) there is a valuable collection of porcelain, rococo mirrors, fans, ancient vases and antiquities. *Mon–Sat 9am–2pm | Via Correale 50 | museocorreale.it | ⏱ 1 hr*

MUSEO ARCHEOLOGICO GEORGES VALLET
The museum in the Piano di Sorrento district is in a beautiful old villa set in the heart of a wonderful park. It displays finds from the prehistoric necropolis and ancient statues found in Roman bathing villas. *Tue, Thu, Sat 9am–1pm, Wed, Fri, Sun 1–6.30pm | Villa Fondi De Sangro | Via Ripa di Cassano | ⏱ 1½ hrs*

EATING & DRINKING

ARTIS DOMUS RELAIS
This is how you imagine a holiday in the south: you can relax, eat well and – even as a non-resident – enjoy the spa in a well-tended villa garden under lemon trees in the centre of town. *June–Aug daily | Via Fuoro 85 | tel. 08 18 77 06 70 | Instagram: artis domusrelaisandspa | €€*

SORRENTO

BAGNI DELFINO
Pure holiday vibes: here you can enjoy delicious seafood dishes at a moderate price on the clifftops by the beach. *April–Oct daily | Via Marina Grande 216 | tel. 08 18 78 20 38 | €€–€€€*

GIGINO PIZZA A METRO
In the neighbouring town of Vico Equense this mega pizzeria (over 100 employees) is famous all over the Gulf of Naples. Historic place with a varied menu. *Daily | Via Nicotera 15 | tel. 08 18 79 84 26 | pizzametro.it | €*

TORRE DEL SARACINO
The highlight of a holiday on the gulf: also in Vico Equense, famed Michelin-starred chef Gennaro Esposito serves the very best Mediterranean cuisine. *Closed Sun evening, Tue lunchtime and Mon | Via Torretta 9 | tel. 08 18 02 85 55 | torredelsaracino.it | €€€*

SHOPPING

The maze of alleyways in the old town (especially *Via San Cesareo* and *Via Fusio*) are full of shops selling jewellery, gemstones, coral and woodwork, small antiques, embroidered tablecloths and leather goods. The evening is a good time to shop in the traffic-calmed centre.

BEACHES

You can access the small, grey-sand beaches and jetties at the foot of the cliff plateau down steep steps and winding pathways. The hotels, which line the cliff edge, have elevators down to the coast or you can take the public elevator at Villa Communale. It is nicest at the fishing village of *Marina Grande*. A beautiful coastline with access to the sea can be found towards *Punta del Capo* and at *Marina di Puolo*. There's a quieter beach at Meta, where you can swim and eat delicious food at the *Giosuè a Mare* beach resort *(April–Aug daily | Via Caruso 2 | tel. 08 18 78 66 85 | giosueamare.it | €€)*.

NIGHTLIFE

The central *Piazza Torquato Tasso* is the main meeting place; from there, stroll

Fruit and veg, leather and jewellery are all for sale on Sorrento's Via San Cesareo

SORRENTO & THE AMALFI COAST

along the Corso Italia and surrounding alleyways that are full of shops which are open late into the night in summer. If you are in the mood for a *tarantella* show, you will enjoy the *Fauno Notte Club* on Piazza Tasso, although it only really gets going after midnight. For unforgettable Sorrento summer evenings, the *Filou Club (Via Santa Maria Pietà 12)* right next to Piazza Tasso has been open for more than three decades. The people of Sorrento love the spontaneously organised evenings with live performances at *Bar Syrenuse (Via Sant'Antonino 14 | barsyrenuse sorrento.it)*.

AROUND SORRENTO

1 MONTE FAITO
18km to the valley station of the cable car, northeast of Sorrento / 35 mins on the SS 145

In the summer months a cable car, *Funivia del Faito (eavsrl.it)*, takes you to the summit of Monte Faito (1,131m), from where there are spectacular views and a belvedere overlooking the Sorrento Peninsula, as well as hikes and outdoor activities. The valley station is the Circumvesuviana station Castellamare di Stabia. If you are afraid of heights, you can take a bus from Vico Equense railway station up to Monte Faito. *E5–6*

2 SANT'AGATA SUI DUE GOLFI
10km south of Sorrento / 20 mins on the SS 145

The gourmet tour continues above Sorrento, with even better views! The village of Sant'Agata (pop. 3,000) has views of both the Gulf of Naples and the Gulf of Salerno and is home to what has been named several times as the best restaurant in Italy: the small but superb ★ 🍽 *Locanda Don Alfonso 1890 (April–Oct Wed–Sun open for dinner, Sat/Sun also open for lunch | Corso Sant'Agata 13 | tel. 08 18 78 00 26 | donalfonso.com | €€€)*. A few steps further and you'll find *Lo Stuzzichino (closed Wed except for June–Aug | Via Deserto 1a | tel. 08 15 33 00 10 | ristorantelostuzzichino.it | €–€€)*, where you can relax as if you were at home with good friends and enjoy a delicious Slow Food meal.

From below Sant'Agata the route goes via Torca to the peaceful fishing bay *Marina di Crapolla*. Further along the SS 145 is *Colli di Fontanelle* and the simple, but good trattoria *Stelluccia (closed Wed in winter | Via Nastro Azzurro 27 | tel. 08 18 08 35 25 | €)* that also serves some tasty vegetarian dishes.

Above Sant'Agata is the organic agrotourism farm *Le Tore (restaurant by arrangement | Via Pontone 43 | tel. 08 18 08 06 37 | letore.com | €–€€)*, which also supplies fruit and vegetables to the Michelin-starred *Quattro Passi* restaurant in Marina del Cantone. On request, they cook for their guests – excellent! There are some lovely hikes that start right outside the front door. *E6*

POSITANO

3 PUNTA CAMPANELLA, NERANO & MARINA DEL CANTONE

13km to Termini, southwest of Sorrento / 25 mins on the coastal road

After busy Sorrento, the route continues at a more leisurely pace through the quiet countryside to the tip of the peninsula at *Punta Campanella (punta campanella.org)*, passing *Massa Lubrense (massalubrenseturismo.it)* with resort hotels, the small, enchanting *Marina della Lobra* fishing port and fantastic hiking trails. Here you should visit one of Sorrento's oldest lemon groves, where they sell excellent *limoncello* and organic citrus oil: Agriturismo La Lobra *(Via Fontanella 17 | lalobra.it)*.

INSIDER TIP Citrus heaven

Thanks to its rich marine life and natural fauna and flora, the Punta Campanella is an *Area Naturale Marina*, a marine sanctuary. From *Termini* you walk to the tip of the cape, with wonderful views of Capri, the ravines and jagged cliffs, both the Salerno and Naples gulfs, and the lighthouse *(there and back in about 3 hrs)*.

INSIDER TIP Coastal hike with knock-out views

The footpath that leads to the secluded, beautiful swimming bay *Baia di Ieranto* starts in *Nerano*. Italians are familiar with the name as the town is famous for its *spaghetti alla nerano*, a creamy pasta with courgettes and provolone. Next is the tranquil fishing village of *Marina del Cantone*, which has a long pebble beach and two famous restaurants: the first is

INSIDER TIP Connoisseur cove

Taverna del Capitano *(closed Mon, Oct–May also Tue | tel. 08 18 08 10 28 | tavernadelcapitano.it | €€€)* right on the beach. The second is the elegant Quattro Passi *(closed Tue evening and Wed except in summer | Via Vespucci 13 | tel. 08 18 08 1271 | ristorante quattropassi.com | €€€)*. *D–E6*

POSITANO

(E6) **A picture-perfect town of cube houses, quaintly stacked on two hills that slope steeply down to the sea. It's a picturesque medley of flat roofs, white, pink and pastel-coloured façades and sun-dappled loggias and balconies woven with bougainvillea and wild roses.**

SORRENTO & THE AMALFI COAST

Out in the bay lies *Li Galli*, a rocky archipelago of small islands, apparently the sirens from the *Odyssey* turned into stone; they were once owned by ballet dancer Rudolf Nureyev, who spent his last summer here. Positano (pop. 3,900) was a fishing village until the 1950s, when it was discovered by the glamorous and the famous, in search of *la dolce vita*. The town boomed and even created its own fashion – *moda positano* – characterised by light, flowing fabrics in Mediterranean colours. Positano is also famous for its art scene and numerous galleries *(liquidartsystem.com)*.

SIGHTSEEING

SANTA MARIA ASSUNTA
This beautiful church with its majolica dome is on the main piazza. On the outside it has, on the tower, a relief by Mimmo Paladino portraying fish and the famous sea monster. *Piazza Flavio Gioia*

EATING & DRINKING

DA ADOLFO 🚩
Beach resort, bar and restaurant rolled into one. Here, fresh fish is served at the water's edge in a picturesque bay – truly romantic in the evening. There's a boat shuttle service from the beach at Positano. *Daily in summer | Via Laurito 40 | tel. 089875022 | daadolfo.com | €€*

LA TAGLIATA
Be sure to book in advance. Chef Peppe invites you to enjoy his seasonal cuisine for a fair fixed price. The trattoria with a dream view high up in

A cascade of houses climbs up the rocky coast above the small town beach at Positano

AROUND POSITANO

Montepertuso offers a delicious dinner menu for 50 euros and a lunch menu for 40 euros. A dozen dishes are served and drinks are also included. Evening shuttle service from Positano. *Mid-March–mid-Nov daily | Montepertuso | Via Tagliata 32b | tel. 0 89 87 58 72 | €€*

MELE PIZZA AND GRILL
This restaurant is somewhat hidden away in a green space by the stream that runs through the village. Delicious cuisine and pizzas. *Closed Wed | Via Vecchia 5 | tel. 0 89 87 52 32 | €€–€€€*

SHOPPING

Positano's centre is a pedestrian zone and its meandering *Via Pasitea* is lined with one boutique after another, all full of colourful summer fashions, sandals and bags. Everything is very casual, elegant and far from cheap. Another option is to buy some of the local specialities: Campania wines, citrus marmalades and *limoncello*, the bright yellow lemon liqueur. The lemon and maquis fragrances of the Costiera Amalfitana are available in perfume from *Profumi di Positano (Via Cristoforo Colombo 175 | profumidipositano.it)*.

SPORT & ACTIVITIES

You can go on wonderful mountain excursions from Positano: a typical tour takes you from Nocelle up a steep climb to the *belvedere* at the small *Santa Maria del Castello* pilgrimage church. One of *La Divina Costiera*'s most beautiful hikes is the *Sentiero degli Dei* mountain trail from Montepertuso via Nocelle to Agerola (see p. 98).

NIGHTLIFE

Music on the rocks *(musicontherocks.it)* – literally! The disco and piano bar are at Marina Grande beach.

AROUND POSITANO

❹ MONTEPERTUSO & SPIAGGIA D'ARIENZO
2km to Montepertuso, northeast of Positano / 40 mins via a stairway

Several mountain excursions are possible from Positano. For example, you can climb up some rather steep steps to *Montepertuso*, a little village with some excellent trattorias and spectacular views, such as *La Tagliata* (see p. 93), *Il Ritrovo* (closed Wed in winter | Piazza Cappella 3 | tel. 0 89 87 54 53 | €€) or *Donna Rosa* (closed Tue and at lunchtime | Via Monsignor Vito Talamo | tel. 0 89 81 18 06 | drpositano.com | €€–€€€).

Another stairway leads down to the Spiaggia d'Arienzo, where the *Arienzo Beach Club (arienzobeachclub.com)* with a good restaurant and private boat shuttle to Positano invites you to relax. Public buses commute between Positano, Montepertuso and Nocelle. ▯▯ *E6*

SORRENTO & THE AMALFI COAST

The Piazza del Duomo with its grand staircase is the heart of Amalfi

AMALFI

(F6) Amalfi is made up of a jumble of white houses, two squares and a main street – all connected by lots of quaint, winding alleyways and stairways. There are also seven churches, a magnificent cathedral, the harbour and the narrow, labyrinthine, medieval passageway, Rua Nova Mercatorum, also known as Via dei Mercanti, which threads its way through the maze of houses.

All of this is crammed in between the sea and the Valle dei Mulini (Valley of Mills) ravine, which goes inland from the rocky shore like a steep-sided funnel. Today, at least 5,000 people live on this narrow stretch. In the Middle Ages, when Amalfi was one of four great maritime republics (the others being Pisa, Genoa and Venice) that controlled the movement of goods between the Orient and Occident with their merchant fleets, it was said to house over 20,000 inhabitants. That was until the city was forced to its knees in 1135 by rival Pisa and landslides and storm surges plunged part of the town into the sea.

The region reinvented itself and turned instead to fishing, crafts, jewellery making and – more importantly – to the lucrative production of paper (learnt from the Arabs), with up to 16 paper mills powered by the valley's torrential mountain streams.

This all changed with the construction of the coastal road in 1832 and the arrival of the first foreigners, artists and writers. Amalfi's two large

AMALFI

Ceiling frescoes in Amalfi's cathedral, which features a mixture of styles

monasteries, both from the 13th century, were converted into magnificent hotels: the Luna and the Cappuccini. And Amalfi became the place where the sensitive and wealthy from the north could sit out the winter, from October through to March.

And today? The confines of its location means that it is unlikely that Amalfi's development will spiral out of control. It does get plenty of visitors but despite its popularity the city has kept its charm and remains the (expensive) backdrop for *la dolce vita*, for (expensive) good food and for the wonderful (free!) spectacle of nature from dawn to dusk.

SIGHTSEEING

DUOMO SANT'ANDREA

At the top of a wide, steep staircase is the town's impressive cathedral. The façade has black and white marble stone and open arches with gables colourfully tiled in mosaics. The church collapsed after a landslide in 1861; only the church tower (1180) with its majolica-tiled minaret-style domes remained standing. The cathedral was faithfully rebuilt, although even before the collapse it had been remodelled several times and the broad, pillared arcade façade hides two churches and a cloister with a melange of style elements that include Arab, Norman and Baroque. The original church is the 10th-century

SORRENTO & THE AMALFI COAST

Cappella del Crocifisso, now free of its Baroque stucco and serving as the attractive *cathedral museum*. The three-aisled main church dates back to the 11th century, when the marine republic was at the height of its wealth and power. It has a *bronze portal* from Constantinople, a masterpiece of Byzantine art that dates back to 1066.

There is also the Baroque-designed crypt with the reliquary of St Andrew, the first Apostle, who is venerated as the patron saint of Amalfi. The 13th-century *Chiostro del Paradiso* (cloister), which has an oriental look and feel with its dual arches, was once the burial place for Amalfi's aristocracy. *Chiostro del Paradiso and Museo del Duomo March–June daily 9am–6.45pm, July–Sept 9am–7.45pm, Oct–Feb 10am–1pm and 2.30–4.30pm | ⓘ 1 hr*

ARSENALE
Down at the harbour, on the *Piazza Flavio Gioia* (named after the inventor of the compass), take a look inside the impressive brick building: once part of a medieval shipyard, today it hosts exhibitions.

MUSEO DELLA CARTA
The famous paper factories in Amalfi, which once supplied the Kingdom of Naples, never made the transition to modernisation at the end of the 19th century and only two workshops have survived to the present day: *Amatruda* and *Antica Cartiera Amalfitana* in

AMALFI

Tramonti both offer the highest-quality craftsmanship. The paper is long-lasting, highly prized by artists and used for rare bibliophile treasures. *March-Oct daily 10am-7pm, Nov-Jan Tue-Sun 10am-5pm | Via delle Cartiere 23 | museodellacarta.it | ⓘ 1 hr*

INSIDER TIP: The magic of hand-made paper

EATING & DRINKING

DONNA STELLA
Long after your visit, your memory of Amalfi will always be linked to this outstanding pizzeria in a lemon grove. The deep-fried specialities are highly recommended. *Closed Tue | Salita d'Ancora 4 | tel. 36 63 68 96 66| €-€€*

PANSA
A traditional café on the Piazza del Duomo, with delicious specialities from lemon cakes to *limoncello*, all made using lemons from their own groves. Also tasty snacks. *Daily | pasticceriapansa.it | €-€€*

SHOPPING

Wonderful writing paper, notebooks, albums made of Amatruda paper, as well as antique views of Amalfi are available at *Antiche Stampe di Amalfi (Piazza Duomo 10)*.

SPORT & ACTIVITIES

HIKING TRAILS
On the Amalfi Coast you will not want to lie on the beach all day long. For many decades, holiday visitors have used the ★ *Antichi Sentieri* (📖 F6), the old mule paths and stairways behind Amalfi, for hikes into the mountains and into a different world. The paths take you along terraces of lemon and orange groves, through forests and ravines, and over hills with small villages, such as Pogerola and Pontone which have fantastic views of the coast.

A classic hike leads into the *Valle dei Mulini* with its ruins of old mills, waterfalls and dense forests; another goes through pretty Atrani up to Ravello. More challenging is a mountain hike into the nature reserve *Valle delle Ferriere*, full of rare plant species (especially ferns). The path has been signposted by the Italian Alpine Club (CAI) and goes up to 1,000m, into an alpine landscape, and is famous for its breathtaking views.

INSIDER TIP: Fairy woods

Best of all is the famous ▶ *Sentiero degli Dei*, which begins in Bomerano, a suburb of Agerola. Bomerano is easy to get to from Amalfi by public bus *(sitabus.it)*. The well-signposted "path of the gods" begins at Piazza Capasso, where you can also shop for a picnic. It takes three hours to hike over the saddle of *Colle La Serra*, through villages such as *Nocelle* and *Montepertuso* and finally down many steps to Positano. You can then return to Amalfi by either bus or boat *(coopsantandrea.com, travelmar.it, lucibello.it)*. Ask for maps at the tourist office or in Amalfi's newsagents, or visit *cartotrekking.com* and *giovis.com*.

SORRENTO & THE AMALFI COAST

BEACHES

There is a small sandy beach at Amalfi; otherwise you can retreat to the bays and jetties or the dark, sandy beaches of neighbouring Atrani.

AROUND AMALFI

5 WESTERN AMALFITANA
10km to Praiano, southwest of Amalfi / 25 mins on the Amalfitana (SS 163)

On the road from Amalfi in the direction of the picturesquely scattered village of *Conca dei Marini*, you stumble upon the access point down into the *Grotta dello Smeraldo* (daily 9am–4.30pm, closed when the sea is rough, info: tel. 0 89 85 70 96), a stalactite cave with emerald-green water measuring 60 × 30m. High up on a cliff above the coast lies the white monastery *Santa Rosa*, whose nuns invented the famous and irresistible *sfogliatella* – pastries made with ricotta and candied fruits (see p. 28).

As your journey continues towards Positano, the coastal road passes over the dramatic *Furore* fjord. **INSIDER TIP — Dramatic scenery** In the past, goods were carried from the ravine-like harbour bay up a miles-long stone staircase to the village of *Furore* on the

The Sentiero degli Dei leads high above the coast, with views as far as Positano

AROUND AMALFI

mountain slopes between terraced vines (good local wine) and lemon groves. Every September during the *muri d'autore*, artists come to transform the house walls into artworks by painting them with colourful scenes. This and the dramatic scenery have made Furore a popular destination.

The cliff-diving competition also causes a sensation. For over 30 years, athletes from all over the world have been coming to this unique fjord in autumn to jump into the depths. There are restaurants worth visiting here, such as the *Hostaria di Bacco (Oct–May closed Tue | tel. 0 89 83 03 60 | baccofurore.it | €–€€)* in the upper part of the village with a cookery school and a select wine cellar. Naturally, they serve the Furore flagship wine *Fiorduva* from the internationally renowned Marisa Cuomo winery.

The villages of *Praiano* – set among gardens and olive groves with the beautiful, majolica-decorated church of *San Gennaro* – and *Vettica Maggiore* are on the sunny ridge of Capo Sottile. An embayment in the coastline between sloping hillsides is the location of *Marina di Praia*, with its beach and diving spots. The former fishing hamlet is home to the fantastic fish restaurant *Alfonso a Mare (daily | Via Marina di Praia | tel. 0 89 87 40 91 | alfonsoamare.it | €€).* F6

6 EASTERN AMALFITANA

6km to Maiori, northeast of Amalfi / 20 mins on the Amalfitana (SS 163)

Alongside Amalfi is *Atrani*, not as expensive but very picturesque with its winding, stepped alleys, well-preserved white Mediterranean houses and quaint squares, such as the enchanting *Piazzetta Umberto I*. The *San Salvatore de Bireto* church has a beautiful, oriental bronze portal from 1087. There are a number of inviting restaurants too, such as the small, fine yet inexpensive slow food restaurant *'a Paranza (daily in summer, otherwise closed Tue | Via Dragone 1 | tel. 0 89 87 18 40 | €€).* Next up are *Minori* and *Maiori*, both situated on small estuaries, with wide sandy

> **INSIDER TIP**
> Idyllic Mediterranean locations

SORRENTO & THE AMALFI COAST

beaches, palm promenades and a more modern tourist infrastructure. In Minori there are also some impressive remains of a Roman villa.

At *Capo d'Orso* (Cape Bear) are the remains of an 11th-century Benedictine abbey and divine views of the Amalfi Coast and the Sorrento Peninsula all the way to Capri. It is followed by the village of *Erchie*, situated deep in a valley gorge with a golden sandy bay which is picturesquely bordered by two promontories with towers. Next is the pretty fishing village of *Cetara* with its *San Pietro* church (majolica-decorated dome) and a beautiful sandy beach behind the tower, with crystal-clear, often turquoise-blue sea. *F-G6*

7 VIETRI SUL MARE

20km northeast of Amalfi / 50 mins on the Amalfitana (SS 163)

The end of the Amalfitana is at *Vietri sul Mare* (pop. 7,800), a town with a proud ceramics heritage that dates back to the time of the Etruscans. It is lined with one shop after another selling colourfully glazed dishes, jugs and vases all stacked up against walls decorated with majolica tiles. Well worth seeing in nearby Raito is the

Clearly the best means of transport on the winding, overcrowded Amalfitana: a Vespa

RAVELLO

ceramics museum (Tue–Sun 9am–3pm), which is housed in the *Torretta Belvedere*, a tower set in the park and gardens that surround the *Villa Guariglia*. It also exhibits works from the so-called "German period", when numerous German ceramics artists came to work in Vietri in the 1920s. The majolica tiling in one of the town's renowned ceramics factories is spectacular: *Ceramiche Artistiche Solimene (Via Madonna degli Angeli 7)*. 🕮 G5

RAVELLO

(🕮 F6) **Elegant Ravello (350m above sea level) is the favourite place for many connoisseurs of the La Divina Costiera. At Atrani the road branches off into the lush Valle del Dragone (Valley of the Dragon).**

The road winds up through forests and past terraces with olives and lemon groves, but especially vines as this coast is where some of the best grapes are grown. On the other side of the valley is Scala, with its large Romanesque cathedral. During the Middle Ages, Ravello had good connections with the Normans and the town prospered and today there is nothing provincial about its 12 churches, convents and villas – despite it only having 2,500 inhabitants. A few world-famous luxury hotels in impressive *palazzi* and enchanting gardens with breathtaking views complete the picture.

SIGHTSEEING

DUOMO SAN PANTALEONE
Work carried out in 1975 restored the original 11th- and 12th-century Romanesque architecture and removed all traces of the Baroque. The influence of the Norman-Byzantine culture is evident in the 12th-century bronze door, in the mosaics of the *ambo* (lectern), and in the mosaics and reliefs on the 13th-century pulpit. The left side altar houses the relics of the town's patron saint, Pantaleone. The small *cathedral museum (daily 9am–7pm)* houses precious reliquaries and the 1272 marble bust of Sigilgaita Rufolo, a member of Ravello's Rufolo dynasty. *Piazza Duomo* | ⏱ *30 mins*

VILLA RUFOLO
A solid entrance tower leads into this medieval villa in an Arab-Sicilian style (evident in the pointed arches in the small courtyard, for example) with its wonderful terraced garden above the coast, with palms, pine trees and lovely views wherever you look. In the 13th century this was the home of the wealthy Rufolo family. The villa became famous after the garden was said to have been the inspiration for Richard Wagner's magical Klingsor garden in his opera *Parsifal*. Prestigious concerts (Wagner and others) are held inside or on the terrace. The highlight is the *Ravello Festival (June–Sept | ravellofestival.com)*. *Daily 9am–8pm* | ⏱ *1 hr*

SORRENTO & THE AMALFI COAST

VILLA CIMBRONE
The villa can be traced back to medieval times. Home to an English lord from 1904, it is well situated right on the edge of the cliff saddle by Ravello. The highlight of the villa's stunning gardens – famously redesigned in the early 20th century by Vita Sackville West, with avenues, hedges, sculptures and little temples – is the lookout terrace ★ *Terrazza dell'Infinito* with a breathtaking panoramic view of the coast. Today, the villa houses an exclusive hotel and a Michelin-starred restaurant. *Park daily 9am–7.30pm | hotelvillacimbrone.com | ⏱ 1 hr*

EATING & DRINKING

CUMPÀ COSIMO
A must for its highly acclaimed, delicious pasta dishes. It has the cosy ambience of a trattoria – but the prices are in a higher category. *Daily | Via Roma 44 | tel. 089 85 71 56 | €€*

SISINA'S SNACKBAR
Tasty *panini* and small appetising snacks served with a view over to the neighbouring community of Scala. *Closed Sun | Piazza Fontana Moresca 2 | tel. 0 89 85 78 54 56 | sisinas.it*

VILLA MARIA
Another dream location with lovely views is the comfortable terrace restaurant of the charming Villa Maria hotel. Fresh traditional cuisine. *Daily | Via Santa Chiara 2 | tel. 0 89 85 72 55 | villamaria.it | €€–€€€*

Surrounded by operatic legend: the terraced garden of Villa Rufolo

The Byzantine influence is unmistakable: mosaics in the Duomo di Salerno

SALERNO

(⬚* G5)* **The port and provincial capital (pop. 135,000) has experienced a revival over the years with its impressive fusion of medieval and 21st-century architecture, the latter designed by renowned architects such as Zaha Hadid** *(Stazione Marittima)*, **Santiago Calatrava** *(Porto Turistico)* **and David Chipperfield** *(Cittadella Giudiziaria).*

The town has hit the headlines for a variety of innovative ideas and projects ranging from its waste organisation scheme to cultural events such as its imaginative Christmas lights installations. The lively old town around *Piazza Cavour* is full of wine bars, trattorias and beautiful shops. It is also full of students, thanks to its acclaimed university, established in the Middle Ages from the prestigious Scuola Medica Salernitana, the world's first medical school.

SIGHTSEEING

DUOMO DI SALERNO ★
When the city – under Robert the Giuscard, the Norman ruler of the southern Italian kingdom – secured the relics of the Apostle Matthew in the 11th century, it had reason to build this impressive basilica with its valuable bronze portal, Byzantine

SORRENTO & THE AMALFI COAST

mosaics and Romanesque masonry. *Mon–Sat 8.30am–7.30pm, Sun 8.30am–1pm and 4–7.30pm | Piazza Alfano Primo 1 | ⓒ 30 mins*

MUSEO DIOCESANO
The showpiece of the Diocesan Museum, above the cathedral, is the large cycle of medieval carved ivory panels. The 67 reliefs depict scenes from the Old and New Testament. *Thu–Tue 9am–1pm and (except for Sat/Sun) 3–7pm | Largo Plebiscito 12 | ⓒ 1 hr*

GIARDINO DELLA MINERVA
The *Giardino della Minerva* in Salerno, a peaceful oasis in the midst of the old town, was where, in the 14th century, the students from Italy's first medical faculty learnt how to heal with herbs and essences. *Closed for renovation work at the time of writing | Vicolo Ferrante Sanseverino 1 | giardinodellaminerva.it | ⓒ 1½ hrs*

INSIDER TIP
Smell the medicinal herbs

CASTELLO DI ARECHI
This imposing medieval fortification is built on top of a hill, with beautiful views over the city. A museum, a chic café and various cultural events fill the castle with life throughout the year. *Tue–Sat 9am–5pm, Sun 9am–3.30pm | ilcastellodiarechi.it | ⓒ 1 hr*

EATING & DRINKING

HOSTARIA IL BRIGANTE
Simple *hosteria* with fresh, creative cuisine and good wines near the cathedral. *Closed Mon | Via Fratelli Linguiti 4 | tel. 38 92 62 57 56 | €*

OSTERIA CANALI
Let Signora Sabrina's dishes melt in your mouth and you will understand the true meaning of "Slow Food"! The emphasis here is on Cilento regional cuisine. *Closed Mon | Via Canali 34 | tel. 33 95 25 26 72 | FB: osteria.canali | €€*

INSIDER TIP
A food lover's paradise

WHERE TO STAY IN SORRENTO & ON THE AMALFI COAST

IT'S PARADISE!
The small family hotel *Alfonso a Mare (14 rooms | Via Marina di Praia | tel. 0 89 87 40 91 | alfonsoamare.it | €–€€)*, which is also a first-class fish restaurant and a beach resort, is located in the enchanting bay of Marina di Praia. Here, you can go on holiday by the sea, just like in the 1960s!

VIEWS OF THE GULF & MOUNT VESUVIUS
The very well-equipped *Villa Ketty (10 rooms | Via Comunale Scrajo 10 | tel. 32 97 34 28 20 | villaketty.com | €–€€)*, with a swimming pool and sea views, is located 10km northeast of Sorrento in Vico Equense. The fruit served at breakfast in this lovingly run B&B comes from their own garden.

PAESTUM & CILENTO

UNSPOILT NATURE & GREAT SEA SWIMMING

Paestum, with its Greek temples, is situated on a broad plain where black buffalo roam, followed by a forested hilly and mountain landscape that stretches down to the coast as far as the Gulf of Policastro.

The coastline, eroded by the sea, wind and rivers, is dotted with rocky capes, grottos and stone arches. There are beaches with fine sand and crystal-clear water, where diving conditions are excellent. Santa Maria di Castellabate and Acciaroli are especially worth

Rocky capes, grottos and bays for swimming: the Gulf of Policastro

discovering. Marina di Camerota and glamorous Palinuro are particularly busy in high season when the Italians are on holiday.

The rural hinterland is wildly romantic, with farming villages, olive groves and vineyards, perfect for hiking, biking and regional food. The Parco Nazionale del Cilento, Vallo di Diano e Alburni *(cilentoediano.it)* and the mountain range of Monti Alburni is now a UNESCO World Heritage Site with cultural treasures such as the ancient temples of Paestum and the Carthusian monastery in Padula.

MARCO POLO HIGHLIGHTS

★ PAESTUM
The best-preserved Greek temples, the most vibrant frescoes of antiquity – and, afterwards, the best fresh buffalo mozzarella ➤ p. 110

★ GROTTE DI CASTELCIVITA
Visit the most spectacular cave in the karst mountains of Cilento ➤ p. 112

★ PUNTA LICOSA
This headland in Castellabate gets you in the mood for long coastal hikes with great views ➤ p. 114

★ BOAT TRIPS
Take a relaxing boat trip to some fantastic sea grottos and then enjoy a barbecue on the beach ➤ p. 116

★ CERTOSA DI SAN LORENZO
The Carthusian monastery of Padula has the largest cloister in the world and is now a UNESCO World Heritage Site ➤ p. 117

★ MARINA DI CAMEROTA COAST
Outdoor pleasures on foot and in a boat: discover the beautiful bathing bays and grottos from a boat and hike along the steep coastline ➤ p. 118

PAESTUM

The Tempio di Nettuno is the best preserved of Paestum's three temples

PAESTUM

(🕮 J8) **In daylight, the majestic temples of ⭐ Paestum have dominated the backdrop of the Cilento Mountains since antiquity. At night, the mighty buildings now look like architecture from the future: a light show bathes the ancient trio in a magical light and creates a futuristic atmosphere.**

Uncovered beneath rampant vegetation in the 18th century, the site turned out to be the centre of a large city founded by the Greeks (sixth century BCE) and colonised by the Romans (third century BCE): three massive, amazingly well-preserved temples: the remains of an amphitheatre, an agora (the Greek assembly square) and the forum (Roman assembly square) as well as thick fortification walls from the fifth century BCE.

SIGHTSEEING

TEMPLES

Of the three temples – which you have to imagine as being brightly painted and decorated with stone ornaments – the best preserved is the middle one (480–470 BCE). Right next to it is the oldest temple (560 BCE) known as the Basilica and supposedly dedicated to Hera. The smallest temple, north of the forum, was probably dedicated to Athena and is also called Ceres Temple. The foundations of a few Roman villas have been exposed in the extensive residential area to the west of the facility. *Daily 8.30am–7.30pm | museo paestum.cultura.gov.it | ⏱ 1½ hrs*

MUSEO ARCHEOLOGICO NAZIONALE 👁

This interesting museum displays items that once adorned the temple city: stone reliefs, terracotta statues,

PAESTUM & CILENTO

painted tombstones and a sensational find: the *tomba del tuffatore*, a tomb with stone slabs depicting a man diving into water from a tower – the image of the symbolic jump from life to death is today used as Paestum's omnipresent logo. *Daily 8.30am–7.30pm | Via Magna Grecia 919 | museopaestum.cultura.gov.it | ⓘ 1½ hrs*

EATING & DRINKING

DOMUS CLELIA

An impressive location, particularly in the evening: be sure to book a table with views overlooking the illuminated Athena Temple. Innovatively prepared Cilento specialities and mouth-watering pizzas are on the menu. *Closed Tue except in summer | Via Magna Graecia 827 | tel. 335 45 56 01 | domusclelia.it | €€–€€€*

RISTORANTE NETTUNO

With fabulous views of the temples, this stylish restaurant boasts delicious dishes – served in summer under the shade of its garden trees. *Closed Mon | Via Nettuno 2 | tel. 08 28 81 10 28 | ristorantenettuno.com | €€€*

TENUTA SELIANO

INSIDER TIP — Buffalo delicacies

This Mediterranean estate has a herd of buffalo whose milk is used to produce the extraordinary mozzarella. *April–Oct daily | Via Seliano 11 | tel. 08 28 72 36 34 | agriturismoseliano.it | €–€€*

SHOPPING

The plain of Paestum is the heartland of the rich, creamy *mozzarella di bufala* cheese and it is also where you can see the black water buffalo in enclosures with ponds. All along the state road 18 towards Battipaglia there are places selling the cheese; a good option is the organic cheese factory *Caseificio Vannulo (Via Galileo Galilei 101 | Capaccio Scalo | vannulo. it)* where you can also buy other buffalo milk products such as yoghurt. Mozzarella can also be bought and tasted in delicious varieties at the beautiful *Lupata* farm *(Via Porta Marina 29 | masserialupata.it)*, which is a ten-minute walk from the temples.

INSIDER TIP — Temples & cheese

Here you can enjoy mozzarella dishes in a marvellous loggia with a view of a cornfield near the excavations. For tasteful souvenirs such as engravings, vases and jewellery, try *Bazar Cerere (Via Magna Graecia 849 | bazarcerere.com)*.

AROUND PAESTUM

🔟 GOLE DEL CALORE

40km east of Paestum / 1 hr via Roccadaspide

The small gorge at the Fiume Calore near Felitto is a hikers' paradise with lots of spots where you can stop and enjoy a refreshing swim. The start and

CASTELLABATE

endpoint of the signposted circular route is the trattoria *Remolino (closed Mon | tel. 08 28 94 53 60 | €)* ==where you can enjoy your fill of home-made pasta and grilled chicken at very reasonable prices.== [INSIDER TIP: Good home cooking] In August, Felitto honours the most famous pasta of Cilento with a big festival: *Sagra del Fusillo Felittese (prolocofelitto.it).* 📖 L8

❷ GROTTE DI CASTELCIVITA ⭐ 🌲 👥
28km northeast of Paestum / 40 mins on the SS 166 and SP 419
This spectacular stalactite cave is part of the remarkable karst cave system of Monti Alburni near Castelcivita in the Calore Valley. With a depth of 4km, it is probably the largest and most diverse of the many caves in Cilento. Guided tours March–Sept daily 10.30am, noon, 1.30pm and 3pm, Oct 10.30am and noon, Nov–Feb on request | grottedicastelcivita.com | ⏱ 1½ hrs | 📖 L7

CASTELLABATE

At the northern tip of Cilento, the municipality (pop. 9,200) consists of three districts *(📖 J9).*

Clinging to the side of the mountain, medieval Castellabate is an endearing place with delightful houses and lanes to explore. Parts of it entail a steep climb and are more enjoyable if you have comfortable shoes. The two other communities are the coastal fishing villages of *Santa Maria di Castellabate* and *San Marco* – both lie on the sandy beaches of Castellabate bay, with the beautiful *Punta Licosa* headland in the south.

At Santa Maria's sandy beach harbour, people meet up in the evening to stroll under the imposing *palazzo* of the noble Perrotti family.

You can eat one metre above the sea on the terrace of the elegant *La Cucina dell'Attore* restaurant *(Mon, Fri, Sun noon–3pm, Tue, Thu 6pm–midnight, Wed, Sat noon–midnight) | Lungomare De Simone 15 | tel. 34 95 46 75 27 | FB: La-Cucina-Dellattore | €€)* with a magnificent view to the horizon. Also in a prime location directly above the beach is the *Osteria del Pozzillo (daily during the summer season | Via Senatore Manente Comunale 1 | tel. 09 74 96 10 01 | osteriadelpozzillo.it | €€).* You can dine on fish dishes at *I Due Fratelli (closed Wed except in summer | Via Sant'Andrea | tel. 09 74 96 80 04 | €–€€),* 1km before Castellabate. *Osteria 1861 (closed Tue | Via Adolfo Cilento 1 | tel. 09 74 96 14 54 | residenzadepoca1861.it | €€)* serves light and elegant Mediterranean cuisine, also in the garden in summer.

The Cilento is famous for its *fichi bianchi* – dried green figs, filled with candied lemon peel and almonds – and the best are available in Santa Maria at *Enoteca Casaburi (Corsa Matarazzo 52).* The owner, Antonio Casaburi, also has some good Cilento travel tips for his clients.

PAESTUM & CILENTO

Gole del Calore: a cool, green oasis away from the crowded beaches in high summer

AROUND CASTELLA BATE

3 AGROPOLI

13km northeast of Castellabate / 25 mins on the SS 267

Every place along the coast has its own individual character. Bustling *Agropoli* has a splendid position and its main street, Corso Garibaldi, is full of shops and cafés. In the old town you can climb up the long flight of steps to the castle which has fantastic views all the way to Capri. One of Agropoli's beaches is the popular *Baia di Trentova,* 2km to the south. There's wonderful hiking on the peninsula between Baia di Trentova and Santa Maria di Castellabate.

You can eat well in Agropoli: the cheese selection is to die for, especially the creamy buffalo mozzarella at *Il Cormorano (closed Wed except in Aug | Via Carlo Pisacane 13 | tel. 09 74 82 39 00 | ristoranteilcormorano.it | €–€€)* at the harbour which is also popular for its fish dishes. Or you can taste the delicious stuffed calamari in the comfortably elegant gourmet restaurant *Il Ceppo (closed Mon except in Aug | Via Madonna del Carmine 31 | tel. 09 74 84 30 36 | hotelristorante ilceppo.com | €€)* on the edge of the village. Why not try one of the top local wines, for example from *Barone*, *Maffini*, *De Conciliis* or *Azienda Agricola San Giovanni (agricolasangiovanni.it)*, which is wonderfully located at Punta Tresino? Popular for disco nights in summer with a magnificent view over the sea is *New Carrubo* on the outskirts of Agropoli. *J8*

AROUND CASTELLABATE

4 PUNTA LICOSA ★
9km to Ogliastro Marina, south of Castellabate / 20 mins on the SS 267
This rugged, maquis-covered headland with the little Isola Licosa off its coast owes its name to Leucosia, one of the three sirens, who waited here for Odysseus. It is a wonderful landscape, with hills sloping down to the sea, fields and olive groves: a bucolic yet naturally wild landscape ideal for hiking. Divers and snorkellers, on the other hand, will enjoy the rocky coast with its clear waters.

In *Ogliastro Marina* (pop. 200) there are a few small hotels – simple, but stylish and with decent rooms – right on the sea that also serve delicious local cuisine, such as *Il Cefalo (daily, booking required | Via Monsignor Passaro 1 | tel. 09 74 96 30 19 | ilcefalo.it | €–€€)* and *Da Carmine (daily | Lungomare Alcide De Gasperi 3 | tel. 09 74 96 30 23 | albergoda carmine.it | €)*. From Ogliastro a pine grove leads down to the headland and a beach. If the access from Ogliastro is closed, you can take another walk (just as nice) to the cape and its lighthouse from the harbour of San Marco di Castellabate. *H9*

5 ACCIAROLI & SAN MAURO CILENTO
22km to Acciaroli, south of Castellabate / 35 mins on the SS 267
After the Punta Licosa headland is Acciaroli with its stately stone houses right on the seafront and its harbour with a large fishing fleet, where wealthy Neapolitans moor their yachts in the summer. From Acciaroli it is on to Pollica, which has fantastic views of the Cilento coast. A culinary tip – in the hills about 12km inland – in *San Mauro Cilento* is *Al Frantoio (daily in summer, otherwise only Fri evenings and Sat/Sun | Ortale | tel. 09 74 90 32 43 | €–€€)*, part of the *Cooperativa Nuovo Cilento (nuovocilento.it)*, which produces one of the best organic olive oils in Campania. The attached restaurant serves authentic regional cuisine. *J9–10*

6 PIOPPI
28km southeast of Castellabate / 45 mins on the SS 267
Further along the coast is the village of Pioppi, which has a pebble beach and cliffs. In the 17th-century Palazzo Vinciprova there's an interesting maritime museum, the ★ *Museo Vivo del Mare (Wed–Mon 10am–12.30pm and 5.30–8.30pm | Via Caracciolo 142 | museovivodelmare.it),* and an exhibition about Mediterranean cuisine. The *La Vela* restaurant *(daily | Via Caracciolo 130 | tel. 32 84 26 38 12 | lavela pioppi.com | €–€€)* has a great location right on the beach, with tables shaded by grapevines. Another good place for some authentic Cilento cooking is *La Caupona (closed Tue except in Aug | Via Antonio Correale 3 | tel. 33 39 09 10 47 | €–€€)*. The owner was a personal friend of the American nutritionist Ancel Keys, who lived in Pioppi when he researched his work on the "Mediterranean diet". The pebbly beaches of Pioppi are among the cleanest in the region.

PAESTUM & CILENTO

The eye-catching Arco Naturale rock arch at Capo Palinuro

7 MARINA DI CASAL VELINO
31km southeast of Castellabate / 50 mins on the SS 267

If you enjoy sitting on the harbour and eating freshly caught fish, then try the restaurant *Trattoria del Mar (closed Mon in winter | Via Angelo Lista 42 | tel. 09 74 35 78 51 | hotelilporto.com | €–€€)* in the town of Marina di Casal Velino. In the hills above is the *I Moresani* holiday farm *(tel. 09 74 90 20 86 | agriturismoimoresani.com | €)* with riding stables and a highly praised Slow Food kitchen. The ingredients are grown on the farm and guests can participate in cooking courses. If you don't like riding, you can use one of their bicycles. *K10*

PALINURO

(L11) **Palinuro takes its name from the helmsman of Aeneas; according to legend he died here in the surf and fierce winds. Virgil wrote about it in the *Aeneid*.**

A legend perhaps, but it does refer to real conditions: the winds around the cape have been difficult for sailors throughout the centuries. The area has a 2,000-year history, as evidenced by the ruins of the settlement of La Molpa on a hill in the southern part of the cape (there are also ruins of a medieval castle here). A short hike leads you there, and it is worth the effort for the breathtaking view. The village of Palinuro (pop. 1,500) itself is only busy in summer.

PALINURO

EATING & DRINKING

AGRITURISMO ISCA DELLE DONNE
Cilento farmhouse cooking with home-grown products which are also for sale: vegetables, salami, cheese, honey, wine and olive oil. It's in an attractive rural setting in Isca delle Donne. *June–Sept daily, otherwise Sat/Sun | tel. 33 84 99 65 11 | iscadelledonne.it | €*

CORE A CORE
For Italians, fish must be served by the sea, and here it is particularly fresh. In summer, you sit in a Mediterranean Garden of Eden. Meat dishes are also served. *Closed Wed lunchtime | Via Fratelli Capozzoli 13 | tel. 09 74 93 16 91 | coreacorepalinuro.it | €–€€*

SHOPPING

The aromatic *miele di corbezzolo* (Cilento honey made from the nectar of the strawberry tree) is available in nearby *San Mauro la Bruca* at *Azienda Agricola Prisco (Valle degli Elci | tel. 09 74974153 | agriturismoprisco.it | €–€€)*. They also serve tasty meals.

SPORT & ACTIVITIES

BOAT TRIPS ★
Boats for hire and boat trips to the surrounding idyllic beaches, rocky bays and coves (only accessible from the sea) or to the spectacular grottos – blue, silver, blood-red – in the limestone coast of the Capo Palinuro. Evening beach barbecues are also available at, for example, *Cooperativa Palinuro Porto (info kiosk at the harbour in summer | palinurocoop.com)*.

The signature dish at Ristorante Angiolina in Pisciotta: *alici alla scapece*, perfect in summer

PAESTUM & CILENTO

BEACHES

Palinuro and Capo Palinuro are surrounded by stunning beaches, including *Baia del Buondormire*, a deep bay with a fine, light-coloured sandy beach and shimmering emerald green sea, *Spiaggia della Marinella* on the south side of the cape and *Cala del Cefalo*.

AROUND PALINURO

8 PISCIOTTA
10km northwest of Palinuro / 15 mins on the coastal road
This hamlet on a hilltop near the sea would be even more picturesque if it were not for the concrete pillars, which tarnish the first impression. Nevertheless, the streets of this medieval old town centre, with its castle and monastery and constantly surprising, magnificent views, have a wonderful atmosphere.

There are several excellent trattorias in the area, such as *Osteria del Borgo (April–Oct daily | Via Roma 17 | tel. 09 74 97 01 13 | €)*, serving delicious food including traditional dishes from the Cilento region. Situated 2km from the centre (shuttle bus available) is the *Enoteca Per Bacco (June–Oct daily, April/May only Fri–Sun | Contrada Marina Campagna 5 | tel. 09 74 97 38 89 | perbacco.it | €–€€)* in an enchanting setting surrounded by olive groves.

This town has a small train station and a fishing village, *Marina di Pisciotta*, down by the sea, which specialises in anchovy fishing *(alici)*. These (and other fish) are deliciously prepared at the Slow Food *Ristorante Angiolina (April–Oct daily | Traversa Passariello 2 | tel. 09 74 97 31 88 | ristoranteangiolina.it | €–€€)* by the sea. Be sure to try the *alici alla scapece*, fried anchovies marinated in vinegar. *L10–11*

9 VELIA
25km northwest of Palinuro / 40 mins on the coastal road
Beyond Ascea are the impressive ruins of Velia (Elea in Greek), once a significant Greek port city. The sprawling archaeological site includes the remains of an acropolis, theatre, thermal baths, residential buildings and the *Porta Rosa* – the only perfectly preserved Greek archway from the fourth century BCE. The site covers an area twice the size of Paestum. *Daily 8.30am–7.30pm | K10*

10 CERTOSA DI SAN LORENZO ★
70km northeast of Palinuro / 1 hr on the SS 517 var
One bend follows another as the road winds its way up into the mountains until it finally straightens out (after about 60km) and enters the *Vallo di Diano* where the wide plains of the River Tanagro are full of fertile fields. In the lovely little town of Padula you'll find the *Certosa di San Lorenzo (Wed–Mon 9am–7.30pm)*, a UNESCO World Heritage Site and the largest Carthusian monastery in Italy,

117

MARINA DI CAMEROTA

founded in 1300. In the 17th century it was vastly extended in an elegant Baroque style: frescoes and wooden and mother-of-pearl inlays decorate the chapels and churches, and majolica tiles adorn the inviting kitchen.

In summer, theatre performances and concerts take place here, and from September there are renowned exhibitions of contemporary art.

At the gates of the monastery, the simple *Trattoria degli Ulivi* (*daily | Viale Certosa | tel. 0 97 57 77 69 | tavolacaldadegliulivi.it | €*) serves local home-cooked dishes and an unforgettable dark red country wine. Padula is famous for its excellent durum wheat bread, and is one of the best places to try it is the Slow Food bakery *L'Antico Forno* (*Via Nazionale 325*) below the town. *N–O8*

MARINA DI CAMEROTA

(*M11–12*) **The road from Palinuro has carved its way through rock promontories flanked by lovely beaches with fine sand on one side and forested mountains rising up on the other.**

Marina di Camerota (pop. 2,600) and Palinuro together form the main holiday area of southern Cilento, and more and more campsites and holiday resorts are springing up in the shadow of the olive trees and pine groves. It is an area of natural beauty and includes the ★ *steep coast of Marina di Camerota* between the Punta degli Infreschi in the south and Capo Palinuro, with its bays, coves and many grottos. A grotto at Mingardo beach is the unusual venue for atmospheric summer disco *Il Ciclope*.

EATING & DRINKING

LA TAVERNA DEL LUPO
Saverio, known as *il lupo* (the wolf), reigns supreme in the enchanting bay of *Spiaggia di Marcellino* in the direction of Scario. Together with his wife and daughter, chef Saverio treats his beach guests to freshly caught fish and delicious wine. Best reached by boat transfer. *June–Sept daily | tel. 33 95 07 55 64 | FB | €–€€*

INSIDER TIP
Fish on the beach

TIRRENO
When the terrace opens in mid-June, the restaurant's location is unbeatable: with a view of the sea and the harbour, the regional dishes taste even better. Local people come here for pizza, especially on Saturdays. *June–mid-Sept daily | Lungomare Trieste 13 | tel. 09 74 93 26 29 | albergotirreno.it | €–€€*

SPORT & ACTIVITIES

You can hike on old mule paths into the mountains and forests in the hinterland, through the rich flora of Cilento, where there is a unique type of primrose, the *primula palinuri*, which only blooms in March/April; it is also the symbol of the national park.

PAESTUM & CILENTO

Or you can hike along the rocky coast and enjoy the wonderful sea views. It is a good idea to have Giacomo Ciociano, a knowledgeable national park guide, accompany you on a tour: *Assitur (Via Duca d'Aosta 19 | tel. 33 86 13 30 20 | FB: Calabianca Calabianca)*.

Excursion boats take you to the sea grottos that dazzle and glimmer with wonderful colours. In summer, the boats *(approx. 20–30 euros)* run regularly to the bays – accessible only from the sea or via long footpaths – from the harbour, where you can find their information counters. Trips with fish barbecue on the beach during the day or in the evening (wonderfully atmospheric) are organised by the fishing cooperative, *Cooperativa Cilento-Mare (tel. 33 36 46 12 40 | coopcilentomare. com)* at the harbour.

You can book fantastic boat tours and guided hikes on *costieradel cilento.it* and *cilentoescursioni.it*. The underwater caves are popular with divers *(continenteblu.com)*, but they are not without danger.

BEACHES

Marina di Camerota has a number of beautiful beaches: a dune beach stretches for miles to the northwest towards Capo Palinuro; stunning *Calanca Bay* lies directly to the west of the town; and sandy *Spiaggia Lentiscelle* stretches east of the harbour. *Cala Bianca* is one of the most beautiful beaches in Italy due to its crystal-clear water. Also, it is rarely crowded as there are no resorts and it is difficult to reach on foot.

Baia degli Infreschi is only accessible by boat or after a long walk

AROUND MARINA DI CAMEROTA

11 BAIA DEGLI INFRESCHI
7km east of Marina di Camerota / 2–2½ hrs on foot or by boat

The hike from *Marina di Camerota* to this wildly romantic bay with its lush, enchanting flora is well-marked and should be easy to follow. The designated starting point is on the western end of magnificent *Lentiscelle Beach*, on the same level as the grotto by the cemetery. It is ideal to combine the tour with a boat ride *(Cooperativa Cilento-Mare | tel. 33 36 46 12 40 | coopcilentomare.com)*. Before you

AROUND MARINA DI CAMEROTA

On the Costa della Masseta, the Cilento coast shows its rugged, more dramatic side

return, stop off at *Oasi Infreschi (April–Oct daily | tel. 34 79 06 64 82 | FB: Baia Degli Infreschi... | €)*. This green oasis is located on a hill overlooking the bay: olives, figs and apples grow here and delicious farmhouse dishes are served. Spontaneous musical interludes are a frequent surprise: every guest can pick up a guitar and tambourine and the Italian guests love to sing. M11–12

INSIDER TIP
Music at lunchtime

12 CAMEROTA & LICUSATI

6km to Camerota north of Marina di Camerota / 10 mins on the SP 66
This old settlement inland is situated picturesquely on a hilltop. From June to September, a *craft market* takes place on Piazza San Vito every Wednesday evening featuring typical products from the region such as earthenware jugs, ceramics, baskets and carvings made from of the wood of olive and carob trees. A legendary pizzeria is named after the classic pizza made with wholemeal flour and oregano: *Rianata a' Vasulata (closed lunchtime | Via San Vito 25 | tel. 09 74 93 54 27 | €)*.

A detour to the village of Licusati above Camerota is worthwhile for the hearty cuisine at *Il Capriccio (daily, Nov–April only Sat/Sun | Via Vincenzo Jervasi 23 | tel. 34 92 65 41 78 | €)*, where they serve delicious Cilento dishes as well as mouthwatering pizzas. Local people swear by the deep-fried seasonal vegetables, *fritto all'italiana* – a crispy delicacy. M11

PAESTUM & CILENTO

13 SCARIO
23km east of Marina di Camerota / 45 mins on the SR 562

On the way to Sapri, a scenic drive with magnificent views of the mountains of Basilicata and Calabria, lies this pretty coastal village with its beautiful church on the piazza and an inviting seaside promenade. There are no beaches in Scario, but that is not a problem as excursion boats commute to beautiful bays along the wild cliffs of the *Costa della Masseta*. 📖 M11

14 SAPRI
37km east of Marina di Camerota / 1 hr on the SR 562

A pleasant coastal town (pop. 6,700) with good beaches, clear water and traditional Campanian cuisine on the central Piazza Plebiscito: *Cantina I Mustazzo (daily | tel. 09 73 60 40 10 | cantinamustazzo.com | €-€€)* and *Cantina R'u Ranco (closed Mon except in July/Aug | tel. 09 73 60 37 06 | locandaariadelre.it | €-€€)*. Sapri is on the Gulf of Policastro on the border of the Basilicata, which begins here with the Maratea coast, one of southern Italy's especially charming coastal areas.

WHERE TO STAY IN CILENTO

BACK IN THE DAY, THE ITALIAN WAY
In the village of Licusati above Camerota, the stately Renaissance *Palazzo Crocco (5 rooms | Largo Crocco | tel. 09 74 93 70 14 | palazzocrocco.it | €)* offers charming, old-fashioned accommodation, and on the adjoining farm it's like being with good friends.

LIKE AN OASIS
The charming *Hotel Marulivo (11 rooms, 3 apartments | Via Castello | tel. 09 74 97 37 92 | marulivohotel.it | €-€€)* in the restored medieval monastery at the foot of the castle in Pisciotta is simply delightful. They organise great activities too: in addition to boat trips, the hotel offers cookery and ceramics courses.

DISCOVERY TOURS

Want to get under the skin of this region? Then our discovery tours are the ideal guide – they provide advice on which sights to visit, tips on where to stop for that perfect holiday snap, a choice of the best places to eat and drink, and suggestions for fun activities.

❶ GOLDEN AGE AROUND CASERTA & CAPUA

- ➤ See how the king lived – behind the scenes at Reggia di Caserta
- ➤ Get on the trail of Spartacus at the amphitheatre
- ➤ Feel fine silk in San Leucio

 Caserta Caserta Vecchia

 approx. 40km 1 day (total driving time 1–1½ hrs)

The best day to take this tour is Thursday: the museum in ❸ **Capua** is only open Tuesday and Thursday afternoons; the palace in ❶ **Caserta** is closed on Tuesdays. Make sure that you book a table at the restaurant in ❻ **Caserta Vecchia**.

The view is spectacular from Villa San Michele in Anacapri

Start your tour in the provincial capital city of ❶ Caserta (pop. 76,000), *approximately 20 minutes' drive from Naples on the A1 northbound towards Rome.* The massive royal palace of the Bourbons, the Reggia di Caserta *(Wed–Mon 8.30am–7.30pm),* is commonly known as the "Versailles of the south". Sprawling over 44,000m², the palace was completed by the Italian-Flemish master builder Luigi Vanvitelli in 1773. Vanvitelli spent over 20 years working on this dream home for the Neapolitan king. Built to showcase grandeur and power, the late-Baroque palace draws almost one million visitors each year and has often been used as a set for films, including one from George Lucas's Star Wars trilogy. The Terrae Motus collection – which was established after the devastating earthquake that hit southern Italy in 1980 – is particularly worth seeing, with works from over 60 contemporary artists, includeing Joseph Beuys, Jannis Kounellis, Gilbert & George and many others.

A WALK IN THE "VERSAILLES OF THE SOUTH"

Do not miss the expansive park gardens *(daily 8.30am– 2 hrs before sunset)* located behind the palace. The long straight avenues and large fountains with tiered water cascades stand in direct contrast to the rambling forests

❶ Caserta

and Caserta's rugged northern mountains. At the far end of the park, the very romantic English Garden comes as a surprises to visitors. The park's long stretches of tarmac avenues invite tourists to explore the gardens by bike (👤 bikes, rickshaws and tandem bikes are available to hire at the park entrance).

SPARTACUS AND BEAN SOUP

After around 20 minutes along the SS 7 you'll reach ❷ Santa Maria Capua Vetere ➤ p. 57, one of the most important cities in Italy during the Roman era. The famous gladiator school, home to Spartacus, was once in its well-maintained amphitheatre (the largest outside Rome at the time). The bean soup, which supposedly turned him into the strong man he was, is served at the excellent organic restaurant Amico Bio Spartacus Arena *(daily | Piazza Adriano | tel. 0 82 31 83 10 93 | FB | €)* right next door to the amphitheatre.

After lunch, your journey takes you *on to Capua through the flat, fertile plain of the Volturno river,* with the impressive volcanic arcs of the Campanian Apennines in the background. Thanks to the mild climate and the rich volcanic soil it has always been the vegetable garden of Campania; the lush, dense vegetation still holds some fascination today, even though it has been spoilt in many areas by ugly urban sprawl. ❸ Capua ➤ p. 57, a

11 km
❷ Santa Maria Capua Vetere

6 km

❸ Capua

DISCOVERY TOURS

Roman settlement on the Via Appia and once the capital city of a Lombard principality, is today a small vibrant town with attractive Baroque façades in the town centre. Do not miss the Museo Campano with its unusual collection of pre-Roman art and cult objects. The district of ❹ Sant'Angelo in Formis ➤ p. 57 *in the northeast* is also worth a visit for its pre-Romanesque Benedictine abbey with splendidly preserved frescoes and its magnificent setting.

SILK SOUVENIRS

Now head along the SP 4 and the SS 87 to ❺ San Leucio, once the famous royal silk factory with the early industrial worker settlement Quartiere San Carlo. Today you can visit the restored royal grounds, the Complesso Monumentale Belvedere San Leucio *(Thu–Tue 9.30am–1.30pm and 3.30–5pm, in winter 3–4.45pm, Wed 9.30am–1.30pm)*, where there's a museum focusing on the silk manufacturing industry, a Baroque garden and fantastic panoramic views over the plains of Caserta. Traditional silk scarves and products are also available in the museum store Antiche Leuciane *(Mon/Tue and Thu–Sat 9.30am–1pm and 4–7pm, Sun 10am–1pm | Piazza Trattoria 1)*.

Return to the SS 87 and head in the direction of Caserta, taking the first left onto Via dei Giardini Reali/Via Gennaro Papa, where you'll reach the picturesque medieval hamlet of ❻ Caserta Vecchia up in the hills. The views across the plain to Mount Vesuvius and the lights of Naples are amazing. With its inviting trattorias and artisan shops, Caserta Vecchia is a popular and vibrant destination, especially at weekends. The perfect finish to this tour is at Gli Scacchi *(closed Mon/Tue | Via Vitagliano Rossetti | tel. 08 23 37 10 86 | €€)*, recommended by the Slow Food guide and located to the east of the town.

6 km
❹ Sant'Angelo in Formis

9 km
❺ San Leucio

10 km
❻ Caserta Vecchia

Late Baroque splendour at Reggia di Caserta

② THROUGH CILENTO'S KARST LANDSCAPE

- Discover a grotto church in the karst limestone mountains
- Ride along the river in unspoilt nature
- Immerse yourself in the Middle Ages in Padula and Teggiano

📍 Polla

→ approx. 250km

🏁 Teggiano

🚗 3 days (total driving time 6–8 hrs)

ℹ️ Book your accommodation and your ride in advance at ❺ AVICA horse club.

DAY 1
❶ Polla
35km
❷ Sant'Angelo a Fasanella
17km
❸ Grotte di Castelcivita
3km
❹ Antico Casolare

DAY 2
21km
❺ AVICA horse club
13km
❻ Roscigno Vecchia
13km
❼ Locanda dell'Angelo

Start your tour in ❶ **Polla** *along a scenic mountain route to* ❷ **Sant'Angelo a Fasanella**, where you can visit the impressive, early medieval San Michele grotto church, with its caves full of altars as well as paintings and frescoes from the 14th/15th century. *Just 15km to the northwest of the church is the equally impressive* ❸ **Grotte di Castelcivita ➤ p. 112**, which is well worth the trip down underground. Spend the night in green surroundings at the delightful ❹ **Antico Casolare** *(agriturismoanticocasolare.it),* where you can enjoy the excellent house wines and honey, jams and olive oil, all produced by the family.

RIDE AND PICNIC ON THE RIVER
Set out the next morning on horseback along the Calore river, *after driving along the SS 488 to Castel San Lorenzo to the* ❺ **AVICA horse club** *(Via Varco della Taverna | tel. 32 90 45 26 77 | trekkingacavallo.it).* This ride includes a delightful picnic break next to the river. *Your route then carries on to* ❻ **Roscigno Vecchia**: take a stroll through this desolate village which had to be evacuated at the beginning of the 20th century due to the danger of landslides. This "19th-century Pompeii" is an interesting excursion in picturesque surroundings. A culinary destination is hidden away in the Valle dell'Angelo: the ❼ **Locanda dell'Angelo** in the middle of the small village offers simple accommodation and a

DISCOVERY TOURS

very warm welcome. Its Slow Food-affiliated Osteria La Piazzetta *(daily | FB: Osteria "La Piazzetta" | €€)* serves refined Cilento cuisine using ingredients from the restaurant's own garden or from local farmers.

WALK TO THE PILGRIMAGE CHURCH ON THE MOUNTAIN

From Novi Velia the road takes you through dense forests up to a height of 1,500m, where it is a short walk to the ❽ Madonna di Novi Velia sanctuary on the holy Monte Sacro mountain (also called Monte Gelbison). This 15th-century church is one of the most important traditional places of worship for Cilento's miners and shepherds. *In Massa, at the junction to Novi Velia, is* ❾ La Chioccia d'Oro *(closed Fri | tel. 0 97 47 00 04 | €)*, which serves tasty, very reasonably priced meals at lunchtime.

The route now winds through Laurito, Rofrano and Sanza to Padula and the large Baroque complex of ❿ Certosa di San Lorenzo ➤ p. 117. In the 15th century, the monks drained the swampy plains of the Vallo di Diano, now a fertile agricultural landscape. The charming, small town of ⓫ Teggiano with castle,

DAY 3

44km

❽ Madonna di Novi Velia

15km

❾ La Chioccia d'Oro

71km

❿ Certosa di San Lorenzo

13km

⓫ Teggiano

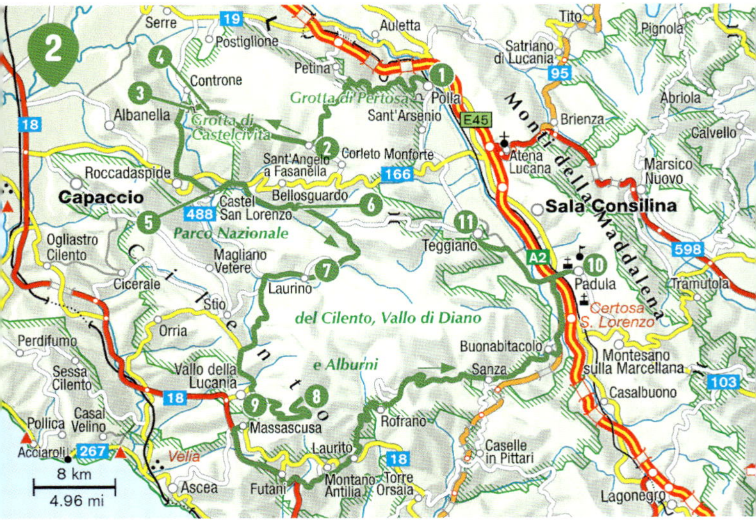

countless churches and stately medieval buildings offers breathtaking views of the surrounding region. Treat yourself at the end of this tour to a memorable stay at the elegant **Antichi Feudi** hotel *(antichifeudi.com)*. The owners have breathed new life into this old baronial palace.

❸ BIRD'S-EYE VIEW FROM CAPRI'S HIGHEST PEAK

- ➤ Enjoy fantastic views across the island to the Gulf of Naples
- ➤ Immerse yourself in the tranquillity of Villa San Michele
- ➤ Swim and chill on the pebble beach

📍 Marina Grande 🏁 Le Ondine
🕐 10km 🥾 1 day (total walking time approx. 3 hrs)
📶 medium

ℹ️ Do not attempt this route on rainy days. If you are unsure about the weather, contact the tourist office *(tel. 08 18 37 06 86)*. Good visibility is essential. To attempt this climb you need a good head for heights, to be physically fit and steady on your feet.

❶ Marina Grande

1,700m

❷ viewpoint

1,300m

From ❶ **Marina Grande** *take the cable car up to the town of Capri. Once you reach the end of Via Roma, take the footpath on the left of the hospital entrance (Via Torina). The path continues steadily uphill. After you leave the town, the path is occasionally signposted in red. After around ten minutes, you'll notice a junction to the right: this leads you to a promontory with olive trees and the first spectacular* ❷ **viewpoint**.

Continue through a holm oak forest. Then comes a stretch of trail with high rocky steps, but soon afterwards you will be treated to the first panoramic views across the island and out to sea. *It is less than half an hour from this point to a high plain near the*

INSIDER TIP
A worthwhile climb

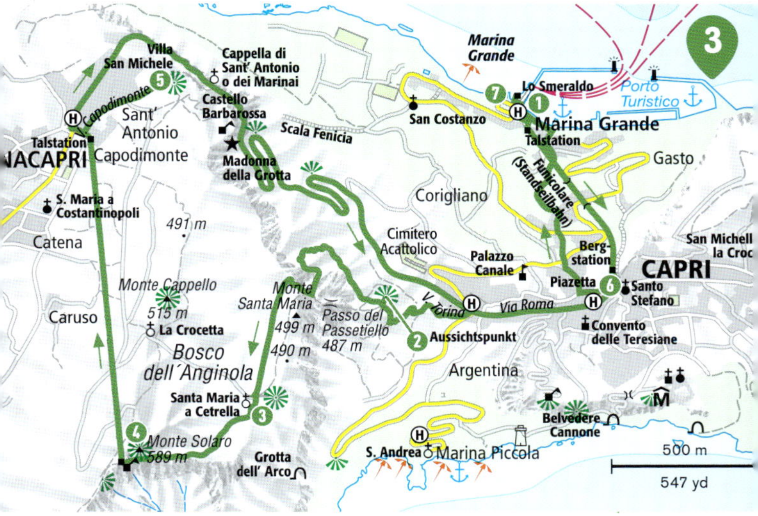

DISCOVERY TOURS

hermitage of ❸ Santa Maria a Cetrella standing at a height of 495m. This paradise setting is the perfect spot for a picnic break.

❸ Santa Maria a Cetrella

TAKE THE CHAIRLIFT DOWNHILL

600m

❹ **Monte Solaro**, the island's highest peak, is now within close reach. *At the top of the mountain you will find the chairlift station from where you can enjoy a comfortable ride down to the centre of Anacapri ➤ p. 77*. Go along the touristy Via Capodimonte with its souvenir shops to ❺ **Villa San Michele ➤ p. 77**, which again offers amazing views of the region.

❹ Monte Solaro

1,600m

❺ Villa San Michele

FINALLY JUMP INTO THE SEA!

3,600m

Returning to Anacapri's Piazza Vittoria, take the bus back to Capri. The bus terminates near the ❻ **Piazzetta**, where you can spot the international jetsetters who gather here in summer. From the base of the Campanile, stroll down the Via Acquaviva set of stairs to the beach in Marina Grande, ❼ **Le Ondine ➤ p. 78**, where you can enjoy the afternoon (sun-)bathing and then in the evening watch the red sun fall into the sea.

❻ Piazzetta

1,100m

❼ Le Ondine

GOOD TO KNOW
HOLIDAY BASICS

ARRIVAL

GETTING THERE
Several airlines fly direct from the UK to Naples airport, Capodichino *(aeroporto dinapoli.it)*, including British Airways *(britishairways.com)*, Alitalia *(alitalia.com)*, Ryanair *(ryanair.com)* Wizz Air *(wizzair.com)* and easyJet *(easyjet.com)*. If you're flying from North America, Australia or New Zealand, you will probably have a stopover in a major city such as London, Paris or Rome.

From the airport to the city centre there is the convenient Alibus *(6am–11.20pm approx. every 15 mins | 5 euros | short.travel/golf24)* which takes 15 minutes to the main railway station *(Stazione Centrale)* and 35 minutes to the harbour (Calata Porta di Massa and Molo Beverello). There is also a bus service from the airport to Sorrento and Cilento (summer only).

There is little advantage to arriving in Naples with your own car. There are car hire companies in Naples, Sorrento and Salerno for excursions, and a car is also practical in Paestum and Cilento.

From the north, the motorway runs from the Brenner Pass via Bologna, Rome, Caserta and Salerno; 1,100km from the Brenner Pass to Palinuro and 800km from Chiasso to Naples.

Travelling by train from the UK involves several changes in Italy, either in Milan or Rome. Naples has three railway stations – Centrale, Mergellina and Campi Flegrei – with hourly connections to Salerno (there is also a bus connection to Salerno, *short.travel/golf25*) and trains from Naples and Salerno to the Cilento coast. A taxi to the city hotels costs about 13 euros.

CLIMATE & WHEN TO GO
High season is from mid-July to the end of August, with a peak around the

A boat trip to the islands or just along the coast is part of a holiday on the Gulf of Naples

Italian public holiday of Ferragosto (15 August): prices for accommodation double or triple during this time; finding a parking space on the Amalfi Coast is practically impossible and temperatures climb above 30 degrees.

The best months to visit are May/June and September to early November. From November to Easter it can be difficult to find open hotels, especially in Cilento. The Amalfi Coast, Capri and Naples are also busy during Christmas and New Year.

GETTING AROUND

CAR
The maximum speed in built-up areas is 50kmh, on main roads 90kmh and 130kmh on motorways (110kmh in the rain). It is mandatory to drive with dipped headlights outside built-up areas during the day. Italy has strict drink-driving laws, only allowing 0.5 alcohol per mil. It is compulsory to carry high-visibility vests in the car. Most highways have a toll fee. Filling stations are generally open Monday to Saturday 7.30am–1.30pm and 3–7pm; motorway service stations are open at all times. Breakdown service: *tel. 80 31 16, from foreign mobiles 8 00 11 68 00 | aci.it*

HIRE CARS
It is highly advisable to book a hire car in advance. In the busy summer months, car hire in the Gulf of Naples can be astronomically expensive.

PUBLIC TRANSPORT
Public transport is reasonably cheap. In Naples there is a good bus network, two underground lines and four cable

cars. Tickets for city buses (currently 1.20 euros for a single journey, 1.40 euros with a change of bus), are available at tobacconists, newspaper kiosks and ticket machines (free with the Campania Artecard). *anm.it*

The Cumana local railway from Montesanto station takes you to Pozzuoli, Baia and Cuma, while the Circumvesuviana from the main station takes you to Herculaneum, Pompeii and Sorrento much more comfortably than by car. *eavsrl.it*

Long-distance coaches to Caserta and Capua *(short.travel/golf17)* depart from Piazza Principe Umberto near the main railway station, and from the port of Molo Beverello (Varco Immacolatella) to Amalfi. The *Cilento Bus (cilentobus.it)* travels to Cilento in summer. *muoversi.regione.campania.it*, *short.travel/golf25*

FERRY CONNECTIONS

Naples has three harbours: hydrofoils *(aliscafi, crossing time approx. 45 mins, single journey approx. 25 euros)* and fast ferries to the islands and to Sorrento, which sail almost hourly during the day in summer, dock at *Molo Beverello (Stazione Marittima)*; car ferries *(traghetti, crossing time approx. 55–85 mins, single journey 12–15 euros)* dock at the *Calata Porta di Massa*. The *aliscafi* to Ischia and Procida leave from Mergellina harbour. There are car ferries from Pozzuoli to Procida and Ischia. The ferry connections between Sorrento and Capri are also good. From Salerno there are ferries to Amalfi and Capri in summer; from Naples and Capri fast boats go to Positano and Amalfi. From April to September there are fast boats to Cilento. The Metrò del Mare connects Naples to Salerno and Capri in July and August, but only on certain days. Always try to buy your tickets online in advance at *capritourism.com* (enter the route, all connections are displayed, and at the bottom of the page you click on the respective ferry company) and collect them on site at the harbour desk. *aliscafi.it, navlib.it, traghettilines.it, capritourism.com, metròdelmare.it*

TAXI

Taxis are relatively cheap in Naples. Unfortunately, there may be sharks at the taxi ranks, especially at the airport and railway station, so it is advisable to call for a taxi *(tel. 0 81 88 88 in English or Italian)*; the easiest way to do this is with the *Goxgo* app. When you are sure about the price, you can relax and enjoy the ride. *taxinapoli.it/en/tariffs*

> **INSIDER TIP**
> **Take a taxi**

RESPONSIBLE TRAVEL

It doesn't take a lot to be environmentally friendly while travelling. Don't just think about your carbon footprint while flying to and from your holiday destination *(myclimate.org, routerank.com)* but also about how you can protect nature and culture abroad: look out for local products, cycle instead of drive, save water, and more. To find out more about ecotourism, please visit: *ecotourism.org*.

GOOD TO KNOW

FESTIVALS & EVENTS
ALL YEAR ROUND

MARCH/APRIL
Good Friday procession (Sorrento), *short.travel/golf22*
Easter procession (Procida, photo), *visitprocida.com*
Pilgrimage to the Madonna dell'Arco (Sant'Anastasia) at Mount Vesuvius (Easter Monday)

APRIL/MAY
Blood miracle of San Gennaro (Duomo San Gennaro, Naples)

MAY
Maggio dei Monumenti (Naples): cultural events, *comune.napoli.it*
Wine & The City (Naples), *wineandthecity.it*

JUNE
I Gigli (Nola): traditional procession of the ancient craft and trade guilds
'La 'Ndrezzata (Buonopane on Ischia): symbolic sword dance
Campania Teatro Festival (Naples and surrounding area), *campaniateatrofestival.it*

JUNE–OCTOBER
Ravello Festival: international music festival, *ravellofestival.com*

A WEEK BETWEEN JULY AND OCTOBER
Pomigliano Jazz (Pomigliano d'Arco), *pomiglianojazz.com*

AUGUST
Ferragosto: parties everywhere
La Notte del Mito (Marina di Camerota): party in the grotto

SEPTEMBER
Blood miracle of San Gennaro (Duomo San Gennaro, Naples)

SEPTEMBER–DECEMBER
Autunno Musicale – Suoni & Luoghi d'Arte (in and around Caserta): a series of concerts, *suonieluoghidarte.com*

DECEMBER
Christmas market (Naples), *short.travel/golf23*

EMERGENCIES

CONSULATES & EMBASSIES
BRITISH EMBASSY
Via Venti Settembre, 80/a, 00187 Rome | tel. +39 06 42 20 00 01 | gov.uk/contact-consulate-rome

UNITED STATES CONSULATE
Piazza della Repubblica, 80122 Naples | tel. +39 08 15 83 81 11 | it.usembassy.gov

EMERGENCY SERVICES
Dial *112* for police, ambulance and fire brigade. Or contact your hotel for help.

ESSENTIALS

ADMISSION FEES
Most major museums and sites charge about 6 euros; entry fees for Pompeii and Ercolano are 18 and 13 euros respectively. It is generally advisable to buy tickets online. Many discounts are available with the 🐷 *Campania Artecard (campaniartecard.it)*, a tourist pass for three or seven days' duration, which can be used for almost all museums and excavation sites in Naples and the region of Campania for free or reduced-price admission, depending on the combination (from 32 euros, 18–25 years from 25 euros). The *Artecard* also includes public transport. It's best to buy it online and collect it once you're in Naples, at *Napoli Official Tour* at the airport or at the central railway station at the *Kiosk Hudson (daily 6am–8pm | platform 22)*, where you can also buy it.

EU citizens under 18 years receive free admission to government museums and sites (18–25 years 50% discount, with ID). Additionally, admission to state museums is free on the first Sunday of each month.

CUSTOMS
EU citizens can import and export goods for their personal use tax-free. Visitors from other countries should check government websites for allowances. Information for UK citizens is available at *gov.uk*.

HOW MUCH IS IT?

Espresso	from 1.10 euros for a cup at the counter
Petrol	around 1.50–1.60 euros for 1L of super
Wine	from 3 euros for a glass of wine
Snack	from 5 euros for a panino
Beach	from 25 euros/day for two sun loungers and a parasol
Bus ride	1.20 euros for a bus or metro ride in Naples

GOOD TO KNOW

NATIONAL HOLIDAYS

1 Jan	*Capodanno* (New Year)
6 Jan	*Epifania* (Epiphany)
March/April	*Pasquetta* (Easter Monday)
25 April	*Liberazione* (Liberation from fascism)
1 May	*Festa del Lavoro* (Labour Day)
2 June	*Festa della Repubblica* (Republic Day)
15 Aug	*Ferragosto* (Assumption Day)
1 Nov	*Ognissanti* (All Saints' Day)
8 Dec	*Immacolata Concezione* (Immaculate Conception)
Dec	*Natale* (Christmas)
Dec	*Santo Stefano* (Boxing Day)

OPENING HOURS

Grocery stores are generally open Monday–Saturday 8.30am–1pm and 5–8pm, supermarkets 8.30am–8pm, small shops 10am–1.30pm and 4.30–8pm. In coastal towns, the shops often stay open until late into the evening. Churches are usually closed 12.30–5pm. Opening hours may change at short notice, so always check the up-to-date times before visiting. Most churches, museums and sights have their opening hours on the internet.

PESCATURISMO

Pescaturismo is going out with a fisherman on his boat, catching fish and preparing them with the fisherman or a cook. Ask for *pescaturismo* at the ports or in tourist information offices.

PHONE & MOBILE PHONE

The country code for Italy is *0039*. It is necessary to dial the whole number, including the *0* at the beginning of each fixed-line connection – both from abroad and when making local calls. UK dialling code: *0044*; US: *001*.

WEATHER IN NAPLES

	JAN	FEB	MARCH	APRIL	MAY	JUNE	JULY	AUG	SEPT	OCT	NOV	DEC
Daytime temperature	11°	12°	15°	18°	22°	27°	29°	29°	26°	21°	17°	13°
Night-time temperature	6°	6°	8°	11°	14°	18°	20°	20°	18°	14°	11°	7°
Hours of sunshine/day	4	4	5	7	8	10	11	10	7	6	5	5
Rainy days/month	10	9	8	7	6	4	2	3	6	9	11	12
Water temperature in °C	14	13	14	15	18	21	24	25	23	21	18	16

USEFUL PHRASES IN ITALIAN

SMALL TALK

We have indicated the stressed vowel by a dot under the vowel.

yes/no/maybe	sì/no/forse
please/thank you	per favore/grazie
Excuse me/sorry!	Scusa!/Scusi!
Pardon?	Come dice?/Prego?
Good morning/good day/good evening/good night!	Buon giorno!/Buon giorno!/Buona sera!/Buona notte!
Hello/Bye/Goodbye!	Ciao!/Ciao!/Arrivederci!
My name is …	Mi chiamo …
What is your name? (formal/informal)	Come si chiama?/Come ti chiami?
I would like … /Do you have …?	Vorrei …/Avete …?
I (don't) like this	(Non) mi piace
good/bad	buono/cattivo

SYMBOLS

EATING & DRINKING

The menu, please	Il menù, per favore
bottle/jug/glass	bottiglia/caraffa/bicchiere
knife/fork/spoon	coltello/forchetta/cucchiaio
salt/pepper/sugar	sale/pepe/zucchero
vinegar/oil/milk/cream/lemon	aceto/olio/latte/panna/limone
with/without ice/fizz (in water)	con/senza ghiaccio/gas
cold/too salty/undercooked	freddo/troppo salato/non cotto
vegetarian/allergy	vegetariano/vegetariana/allergia
I would like to pay, please	Vorrei pagare, per favore
bill/receipt/tip	conto/ricevuta/mancia
cash/debit card/credit card	in contanti/carta di debito/carta di credito

MISCELLANEOUS

Where can I find ... ?	Dove posso trovare ...?
left/right/straight	sinistra/destra/dritto
What time is it?	Che ora è? Che ore sono?
it's three o'clock/ it's half three	Sono le tre./Sono le tre e mezza
today/tomorrow/yesterday	oggi/domani/ieri
How much is ...?	Quanto costa ...?
too much/much/little/everything/nothing	troppo/molto/poco/tutto/niente
expensive/cheap/price	caro/economico/prezzo
Where can I get internet/WiFi?	Dove trovo un accesso internet/wi-fi?
open/closed	aperto/chiuso
broken/it's not working	guasto/non funziona
broken down/garage	guasto/officina
schedule/tickets	orario/biglietto
train/tracks/platform	treno/binario/banchina
Help!/Look out!/Be careful!	Aiuto!/Attenzione!/Prudenza!
ban/forbidden/danger/dangerous	divieto/vietato/pericolo/pericoloso
pharmacy/drug store	farmacia
fever/pain	febbre/dolori
0/1/2/3/4/5/6/7/8/9/10/100/1000	zero/uno/due/tre/quattro/cinque/sei/sette/otto/nove/dieci/cento/mille

HOLIDAY VIBES
FOR RELAXATION & CHILLING

FOR BOOKWORMS & FILM BUFFS

🎥 CAPRI-REVOLUTION
Neapolitan director Mario Martone portrays Capri at the turn of the 20th century. Influenced by foreign visitors to the island, a young goatherd decides to free herself from the shackles of island traditions (2018).

📖 THE TEMPTATION TO BE HAPPY
Lorenzo Marone's novel tells the story of the frustrated 77-year-old Cesare. A charmingly poetic book which provides revealing insights into Neapolitan philosophy. And readers will be captivated by the character of the protagonist (2015).

🎥 NAPOLI VELATA (VEILED NAPLES)
Thriller by director and Italian-by-choice Ferzan Özpetek, which wonderfully portrays the colourful everyday life of Naples, a modern metropolis in which the past is omnipresent in the city's ambience, architecture and lives of the Neapolitans (2017).

📖 GOMORRAH
In an explosive mixture of reportage and novel; journalist Roberto Saviano gives his insights into the economic network of the Camorra. 2008 Winner of the Cannes Grand Prix.

PLAYLIST ON SHUFFLE

0:58

▮ **PINO DANIELE** – NAPUL'È
An iconic song that real Neapolitans know by heart. A tribute to Naples.

▶ **BISEO SANJUST QUARTET** – 'O SURDATO 'NNAMMURATO
A Neapolitan jazz version of the world-famous song.

▶ **IL VOLO** – O SOLE MIO
A young tenor-baritone trio has revitalised this classic.

▶ **NUOVA COMPAGNIA DI CANTO POPOLARE** – TAMMURRIATA NERA
Rhythmical folk song which is also great for dancing.

▶ **LIBERATO** – JE TE VOGLIO BENE ASSAJE
The iconic singer mixes American hip-hop with Neapolitan lyrics.

▶ **LUCA BLINDO** – ITALIANO FIERO
Young singer who, between rap and pop, picks up on current topics popular with young Neapolitans.

Your holiday soundtrack is available on **Spotify** under **MARCO POLO Italy**

Or scan this code with the Spotify app

ONLINE

INCAMPANIA.COM
Official cultural and tourism site of the region of Campania, with an events calendar.

SHORT.TRAVEL/GOLF3
This black-and-white footage shows the Vesuvius eruption of 1944 with English commentary.

SHORT.TRAVEL/GOLF16
Time travel to ancient Pompeii: a virtual reconstruction of the city near Mount Vesuvius that was buried after the eruption of CE 79.

CIAOAMALFI.COM
A good website to explore for travel tips and inspiration, this blog is written by an expat writer and art historian, with entertaining snippets about daily life on the Amalfi Coast.

CAPRI.NET/EN/E/CAPRI-E-IL-CINEMA
Article about movies shot on Capri with the likes of Sophia Loren, Clark Gable, Brigitte Bardot, Marcello Mastroianni and Claudia Cardinale.

TRAVEL PURSUIT
THE MARCO POLO HOLIDAY QUIZ

Do you know your facts about Naples and the Amalfi Coast? Here you can test your knowledge of the little secrets and idiosyncrasies of this region and its people. You will find the correct answers below, with details on pages 18 to 23 of this guide.

❶ What miracle does Naples' patron saint San Gennaro perform?
a) On his name day, it rains 81% of the time in Naples, a city with little rainfall
b) His blood liquefies three times a year
c) He brings Christmas presents to Neapolitan children on 3 January

❷ What is Via San Gregorio Armeno in Naples' historic centre famous for?
a) Diego Maradona, who is still adored by fans today, used to live here
b) Christmas crib figurines are sold here all year round
c) The first pizza is said to have been baked in a bakery here in 1821

❸ What is the name of the iconic singer from Naples who died in 2015?
a) Pino Daniele
b) Lucio Dalla
c) Gigi D'Alessio

❹ In which country was the song "O Sole Mio" composed?
a) Italy
b) Russia
c) USA

❺ Whoever orders a *caffè sospeso* in the bar ...
a) does a good deed
b) gets an espresso with a shot of liqueur or grappa
c) is served with a puff pastry *sfogliatella*

Answers: : 1b, 2b, 3a, 4b, 5a, 6c, 7a, 8c, 9a, 10b, 11a

How can you do a good deed while enjoying a cup of coffee? See question 5

❻ What is the Terra dei Fuochi, the "Land of Fire"?
a) The particularly fertile lava soil on the slopes of Mount Vesuvius
b) The colloquial term for the volcanic Campi Flegrei around Cuma in northern Naples
c) An area in Campania where the Camorra illegally burns toxic waste

❼ Who was Giuseppe Sammartino?
a) A Neapolitan sculptor
b) An SSC Napoli player who scored more goals for the Italian national team than any other player
c) The composer of "O Sole Mio"

❽ What is Libera?
a) A sculpture erected in the historic centre of Naples in 2019
b) A delicacy from the Amalfi Coast
c) An anti-Mafia organisation

❾ What is a book of numbers assigned to dreams and events used for in Naples?
a) To play the lottery
b) To play the popular local board game *Smorfia*
c) For horse betting

❿ What is special about a Neapolitan nativity scene?
a) The figures can only be carved from olive wood
b) The focus is not on the birth of Jesus, but on everyday Neapolitan life
c) It is a UNESCO World Heritage Site

⓫ How do Neapolitans describe Slow Food products that grow or are produced in the region?
a) Zero kilometres
b) From the neighbour's garden
c) Healthy and pollution-free on the table

INDEX

Acciaroli 106, 114
Agerola 94, 98
Agropoli 35, 113
Amalfi 23, 30, 31, 95-99
Amalfitana 85, 99, 100
Anacapri, Capri 73, 76, 77, 129
Antichi Sentieri 98
Arsenale, Amalfi 97
Atrani 99, 100
Baia 8, 35, 56, 132
Baia degli Infreschi 119
Baia del Buondormire 117
Baia di Ieranto 92
Baia di Trentova 113
Blue Grotto (Grotta Azzurra), Capri 72, 76
Bomerano 98
Cala Bianca 119
Cala del Cefalo 117
Calanca Bay 119
Calata Porta di Massa 55, 130
Camerota 120
Campania Artecard 9, 134
Campi Flegrei 55, 56, 63
Capaccio Scalo 32
Capo d'Orso 101
Capo Miseno 56
Capo Palinuro 115, 116, 117, 118, 119
Capo Sottile 100
Capri 16, 32, 72, 76-79, 128-129, 138
Capua 57, 122, 124
Caserta 21, 42, 122, 123, 133
Caserta Vecchia 122, 125
catacombs 8, 50
Certosa di San Lorenzo 117, 127
Cetara 28, 35, 101
Colle La Serra 98
Conca dei Marini 99
Costa della Masseta 120, 121
Cuma 57
Erchie 101
Ercolano 31, 64-66
Felitto 34, 112
Formis 57
Furore 99
Gole del Calore 34, 111
Golfo di Policastro 106, 121
Gragnano 31
Grotta dello Smeraldo 99
Grotta dello Zaffiro 34
Grotte di Castelcivita 8, 112, 126
Herculaneum 15, 58, 64-66
Ischia 16, 28, 32, 33, 72, 73, 79-82, 133
Isola Licosa 114

Licusati 120, 121
Li Galli 93
Madonna di Novi Velia 33, 127
Maiori 100
Marina del Cantone 91, 92
Marina della Lobra 92
Marina di Ascea 32
Marina di Camerota 32, 107, 118, 119, 133
Marina di Casal Velino 35, 115
Marina di Crapolla 91
Marina di Praia 105
Marina di Puolo 90
Massa Lubrense 34, 85
Meta 90
Mingardo 118
Mingardo river 34
Minori 100
Monte Cervati 33
Monte Epomeo 33
Monte Faito 33, 91
Monte Gelbison 33
Montepertuso 94, 98
Monte Sacro 33, 127
Monte Solaro 129
Monte Soprano 33
Monti Alburni 33, 107, 112
Monti Lattari 33, 84
Naples 38-55
Nerano 92
Nocelle 94, 98
Nola 133
Novi Velia 127
Ogliastro Marina 114
Oplontis 15
Osservatorio Vesuviano 63, 68
Padula 107, 117
Paestum 16, 23, 32, 34, 35, 106, 107, 110-111
Palinuro 32, 35, 107, 115
Parco Nazionale del Cilento, Vallo di Diano e Alburni 107
Pioppi 114
Pisciotta 23, 28, 117, 121
Polla 126
Pollica 23, 114
Pompeii 14, 15, 58, 59, 62, 63, 68-71
Porta Nolana 53
Portici 42, 66
Positano 23, 31, 85, 92-94
Pozzuoli 56
Praiano 100
Procida 16, 33, 72, 82-83, 133
Punta Campanella 16, 34, 92
Punta degli Infreschi 118
Punta del Capo 34, 90

Punta Licosa 112, 114
Punta Tragara 73
Quartiere San Carlo 125
Raito 101-102
Ravello 102-103, 133
Reggia di Caserta 10, 123
Rione Terra 56
Roscigno Vecchia 126
Salerno 16, 104-105, 130, 132
San Leucio 31, 125
San Lorenzo monastery 8
San Marco di Castellabate 114
San Mauro Cilento 114
Sant'Agata sui Due Golfi 91
Santa Maria Capua Vetere 52, 57, 124
Santa Maria del Castello 94
Santa Maria di Castellabate 106, 112, 113
Sant'Angelo 73
Sant'Angelo a Fasanella 126
Sant'Angelo in Formis 57, 125
Santa Rosa monastery 99
Santuario della Madonna del Rosario 68
Sapri 121
Scala 102
Scario 121
Sentiero degli Dei 11, 94, 98
Sorgeto Bay 9
Sorrento 30, 31, 88-91, 133
Spiaggia d'Arienzo 94
Spiaggia della Marinella 117
Spiaggia Lentiscelle 119
Stabiae 62, 67
Teatro San Carlo 42, 54
Teggiano 127
Termini 92
Torre Annunziata 71
Tramonti 31, 98
Valle dei Mulini 98
Valle del Dragone 102
Valle dell'Angelo 126
Valle delle Ferriere 98
Vallo di Diano 34, 117, 127
Velia (Elea) 117
Vesuvius, Mount 14, 22, 26, 28, 62, 63, 67-68, 133
Vettica Maggiore 100
Vico Equense 90, 91, 105
Vietri sul Mare 84, 101
Villa Campolieto 66
Villa dei Papiri 66
Villa Favorita 66
Villa Oplontis 71
Villa Petti Ruggiero 66
Ville Vesuviane 66
Vivara 83

INDEX & CREDITS

WE WANT TO HEAR FROM YOU!

Did you have a great holiday? Is there something on your mind? Whatever it is, let us know! Whether you want to praise the guide, alert us to errors or give us a personal tip – MARCO POLO would be pleased to hear from you. Please contact us by email:

sales@heartwoodpublishing.co.uk

We do everything we can to provide the very latest information for your trip. Nevertheless, despite all of our authors' thorough research, errors can creep in. MARCO POLO does not accept any liability for this.

PICTURE CREDITS
Cover photo: Praiano, Kirche San Gennaro (AWL Images/imagebroker)
Photos: huber-images: M. Borchi (138/139), M. Bortoli (6/7), P. Canali (72/73, 84/85, 122/123), A. Capone (8), M. Carassale (11, 53), C. Dörr (76), D. Erbetta (32/33, 81), G. Filippini (79), G. Greco (26/27), D. Iemma (120/121), Kaos01 (65), S. Kremer (30/31, 92/93, 95), S. Lubenow (38/39, 46), S. Scatà (27), G. Simeone (12/13, 115); Laif: F. Blickle (130/131), R. Celentano (35, 99), F. Heuer (100/101, 106/107), Jonkmanns (20), M. Kirchgessner (116), B. Morandi (55), G. Piscitelli (9), D. Schmid (45), D. Schwelle (43), Standl (119); Laif/Archivolatino: Moscia (58/59); Laif/Redux/The New York Times: G. Cipriano (50); Laif/robertharding: F. Fell (90), E. Scriven (2/3); Look: K. Johaentges (140/141), S. Lubenow (88/89), K. Wothe (14/15, 70, 110, 113); Look/ClickAlps (24/25); mauritius images: B. Kickner (18/19); mauritius images/Alamy: (56), S. Armaroli (63), S. Crespiatico (125), F. Sciarra (133); mauritius images/ClickAlps (back cover flap, 103); mauritius images/CuboImages (31, 49, 82, 104); mauritius images/euroluftbild.de (67); mauritius images/imagebroker: U. Kraft (outer front cover flap, inner front cover flap/1), M. Moxter (96/97); mauritius images/Westend61 (10); picture-alliance/EPA-EFE: ANSA (22); S. Sonnentag (143)

4th Edition – fully revised and updated 2024
Worldwide Distribution: Heartwood Publishing Ltd, Bath, United Kingdom
www.heartwoodpublishing.co.uk

Authors: Bettina Dürr, Stefanie Sonnentag
Editor: Nikolai Michaelis
Picture editor: Anja Schlatterer

Cartography: © MAIRDUMONT, Ostfildern (pp. 36–37, 64, 69, 124, 127, 129, pull-out map; Kompass Karten GmbH, A-Innsbruck; © MAIRDUMONT, Ostfildern, using data from OpenStreetMap, licence CC-BY-SA 2.0 (pp. 40–41, 60–61, 74–75, 86–87, 108–109)
Cover design and pull-out map cover design: bilekjaeger_Kreativagentur with Zukunftswerkstatt, Stuttgart
Page design: Langenstein Communication GmbH, Ludwigsburg

Heartwood Publishing credits:
Translated from the German by Thomas Moser, Susan Jones
Editors: Felicity Laughton, Kate Michell, Rosamund Sales
Prepress: Summerlane Books, Bath
Printed in India

MARCO POLO AUTHOR
STEFANIE SONNENTAG
You can't always rely on listed opening hours, the bureaucracy can be infuriating at times and certain things don't work as smoothly as they do in the North – but Neapolitans always find a creative solution. Their warmth, their everyday spontaneity, the magical silhouette of Mount Vesuvius and the soft light of the Mediterranean sun are unrivalled: art historian (PhD) and author Stefanie just loves living in Naples.

DOS & DON'TS

HOW TO AVOID SLIP-UPS & BLUNDERS

DON'T PICK THE LEMONS
Please don't pick fruit while hiking through the lemon groves and vineyards – the farmers work hard and this is their source of income.

DON'T FORGET YOUR SWIM SHOES, SNORKEL & MASK
Plastic sandals are a must for getting into the sea as access is often over rocks, stones or down concrete steps. A mask and snorkel are essential for an exciting view into the underwater world around the rocky coast.

AVOID DRIVING A CAR
Busy roads are best avoided in Naples, on the Sorrento Peninsula and the Amalfitana coastal road (especially in summer and at weekends, when the Neapolitans are also out and about). There is no parking to be found. Instead, use public transport. In Naples, only residents can access the old town by car.

DON'T PAY JUST FOR YOURSELF
If you're travelling with Neapolitans, asking for a separate bill will be frowned upon! At the bar, sometimes one person pays, sometimes the other, and at the trattoria it's *alla romana*: the bill, including tips, is shared between everyone.

DO STAY ALERT
Be careful and alert on crowded buses, underground trains and the Circumvesuviana and Cumana trains. Don't wear flashy jewellery and have your phone safely tucked away. Turn your bag opening inwards, keep your money and documents under your clothes and always lock your doors when driving.